Leading
Academic Achievement
FOR
English Language Learners

Dedication

This book is dedicated to my wonderful father,
Edward Thompson (1917–2010), who appreciated life each day
and exemplified caring, character, and love throughout his life.
He served as a model of how life can be lived to the fullest
and have its deepest meaning. Thank you, Daddy.

—Betty J. Alford

For my students—past, present, and future.

—Mary Catherine Niño

Leading
Academic Achievement
FOR
English Language Learners

A GUIDE FOR PRINCIPALS

A Joint Publication

learning forward
CORWIN
A SAGE Company

Betty J. Alford
Mary Catherine Niño

CORWIN
A SAGE Company

FOR INFORMATION:

Corwin
A SAGE Company
2455 Teller Road
Thousand Oaks, California 91320
(800) 233-9936
Fax: (800) 417-2466
www.corwin.com

SAGE Ltd.
1 Oliver's Yard
55 City Road
London EC1Y 1SP
United Kingdom

SAGE India Pvt. Ltd.
B 1/I 1 Mohan Cooperative Industrial Area
Mathura Road, New Delhi 110 044
India

SAGE Asia-Pacific Pte. Ltd.
33 Pekin Street #02-01
Far East Square
Singapore 048763

Acquisitions Editor: Debra Stollenwerk
Associate Editor: Desirée Bartlett
Editorial Assistant: Kimberly Greenberg
Production Editor: Amy Schroller
Copy Editor: Barbara Corrigan
Typesetter: C&M Digitals (P) Ltd.
Proofreader: Sally Jaskold
Indexer: Maria Sosnowski
Cover Designer: Rose Storey
Permissions Editor: Adele Hutchinson

Copyright © 2011 by Corwin

Printed in the United States of America

Library of Congress Cataloging-in-Publication Data

Alford, Betty J.

Leading academic achievement for English language learners : a guide for principals / Betty J. Alford, Mary Catherine Niño.

p. cm.
"A Joint Publication With Learning Forward."

Includes bibliographical references.

ISBN 978-1-4129-8160-6 (pbk. : alk. paper)

1. English language—Study and teaching—Foreign speakers. 2. Multilingualism in children. 3. Educational leadership. 4. School principals. 5. Academic achievement. I. Niño, Mary Catherine. II. Title.

PE1128.A2A36 2011 428.2'4071—dc22 2011001807

This book is printed on acid-free paper.

14 15 16 17 18 10 9 8 7 6 5 4 3 2

Contents

Preface

Educators are all too familiar with the statistics related to English language learners (ELLs), and it seems that news headlines frequently offer grim predictions for schools with large ELL populations. However, if we as educational leaders let these quips and bylines guide our vision, then our students are going to drop out, never learn English, and fail to meet minimum standards—and we will be left with some explaining to do.

Negative outcomes are not, and do not have to be, the reality for ELLs. While education statistics can be used to paint a grim picture, these statistics must be considered within the context of the larger educational and demographic landscape. In this book, we advance that leadership can yield positive results for ELLs. We offer you the voices of school leaders who are making a positive difference in meeting the needs of ELLs and hope their examples will help us all to foster the academic achievement and language acquisition of ELLs.

This book examines successful leadership practices and strategies, embedded professional development methods, and implementation models that build both a culture of high expectations for ELLs and teacher capacity to scaffold students to levels of high achievement while simultaneously helping students develop the English language. This is no easy task. It requires systemic and systematic leadership, comprehensive planning, continuous support, a culture of collaboration, and myriad other generic leadership skills. Building and sustaining a culture of high expectations and achievement for ELLs requires attention to and knowledge of language acquisition processes and home cultures. Infusing this knowledge into one's leadership processes requires drawing together content-area stakeholders who may never have worked together—such as English as a second language and core teachers—and drawing together community members who may never before have been invited to the proverbial table.

This book addresses the issues that confront school leaders as they implement best practices for ELLs. While best practices for ELLs have been identified in the knowledge base, additional examples of the instructional leader's role in implementing best practices at the campus level are needed. In addition, the nuanced nature of the educational change process as it relates to the issue of improving instruction and raising academic expectations for ELLs has not been fully addressed. This book discusses how to engage explicitly in campus-level change efforts to improve learning for ELLs, the knowledge school leaders need, and how to share that knowledge with faculty through professional development. This book also identifies the specific cultural needs of students and how campuses can meet those needs by partnering with the community, parents, and students themselves. This book provides school leaders knowledge and tools to meet the needs of ELLs on their campuses. This approach is based on the model of distributive leadership and the pivotal role of the instructional leader as the leader of learners.

ORGANIZATION OF THE BOOK

Chapter 1, "Preparing for Success: Strengthening a Culture of Academic Achievement for English Language Learners," briefly establishes the need for principals to explore their roles as the instructional leaders of ELLs based on demographic information and introductory information about ELLs in American schools. Next, critical practices for the school principal are introduced: building shared values, building positive relationships, fostering conditions to support learning, and celebrating academic success. The chapter concludes with a case study vignette to guide questions for discussion or reflection.

Chapter 2, "Advocating for Student Success," outlines the principal's practices for ELL student success. This process is guided by reflecting on data—both quantitative assessment data and qualitative data elicited from stakeholder voices. The chapter explores suggestions for gaining the qualitative data by building meaningful relationships through *confianza*—a combination of trust, mutual respect, comfort, familiarity, and understanding based on experience, which yields mutual confidence among all stakeholders. The chapter offers structures for successful and effective use of relationships, including structures for peer coaching, professional collaboration, and meaningful, supportive interactions.

Chapter 3, "Strengthening Knowledge of Second Language Acquisition," provides practical information concerning the principal's role in strengthening the principal's and faculty's knowledge base. Critical knowledge related to ELLs, including language acquisition and linguistic theory, is presented in relevant, applicable, and understandable ways. Then, the chapter provides straightforward ways for principals to apply this knowledge to their own practice as well as their teachers' practice. The chapter offers warnings against deficit thinking related to the abilities of ELLs and their perceived cultural or social needs. This warning is met with a practical guide for ways principals can challenge common assumptions about ELLs. Current laws and current court cases related to equitable school experiences for ELLs are examined. A case study and reflection questions are offered to help readers apply the chapter's content.

Chapter 4, "The Principal's Role in Building Capacity in the School Through Quality Professional Development," explains the principal's role in building capacity in the school through quality professional development. This chapter offers ways for principals to assess specific faculty professional development needs and identifies common faculty needs as a starting point for exploration. Next, the chapter helps principals build the skills needed to solidify faculty commitment to ELLs' attainment of academic content at high levels. A content-embedded case study provides practical examples of quality professional development, including sustained, embedded, and content-specific professional development opportunities. The case study elicits voices of school principals as a platform for reflection questions.

Chapter 5, "Strengthening Home-School-Community-University Connections," focuses on the principal's role in strengthening home-school connections. Practical suggestions for encouraging parental involvement, providing outreach and support to empower community stakeholders to build the culture of high expectations for ELLs, and facilitating a school-university-home-community partnership are explored. The chapter provides advice for establishing partnerships with school and community social workers and staying current on community issues that affect student learning and parental involvement (i.e., immigration concerns). In addition, the chapter provides structures for establishing postsecondary opportunities for ELLs. The case study and questions provide a context for principals to explore the critical elements of a successful school-university-community-parent partnership.

Chapter 6, "Resources for School Improvement in Meeting the Needs of English Language Learners," provides an overview of resources for principals engaged in instructional improvement for ELLs. Books, websites, and other suggested materials are recommended as well.

Special Materials

- **Case Studies:** This book includes cases describing school leaders' situations, decisions, and actions related to leading positive change for ELLs on their campuses. These cases are followed by questions meant to foster critical dialogue or reflection as readers seek to apply the concepts from each chapter. The cases are based on two years of case study research of teachers, teacher leaders, and instructional leaders who were engaged in a change effort for instructional improvement for ELLs and six years of case study research of a school-university-community partnership designed to increase the college-going rates of students.

- **Action Points:** Action points describe steps that instructional leaders have taken in difficult situations. These are implementable actions that move ideas from theory to practice.
- **Consider This:** This section uses questions to bring critical issues to the forefront. The purpose of Consider This is to explicitly address points the principal must assess regarding his or her specific faculty and campus needs. In addition, Consider This provides easy-to-reference statistics, points, and other information for principals to use with faculty. Consider This also provides focus or discussion questions.
- **Straight Talk From the Field:** Principals share their first-person perspectives on issues related to the content of each chapter.
- **Tools:** Tools to guide principals in implementing concepts are aligned with the concepts from each chapter and are included at the back of the book for easy reference. Tools are generally in chart format and provide easy-to-read summaries of information as well as implications for practice. These tools guide principals quickly to action and provide easy reference for faculty meetings, observations, and other principal practices.

Acknowledgments

Authors' Acknowledgments

We express our appreciation to our wonderful English Language Acquisition Center of Excellence and East Texas Gaining Early Awareness and Readiness for Undergraduate Programs partners as well as to the other outstanding educators we have met during our ten years of school-university-partnership work. Their passionate commitment to educational excellence and equity contributes to the attainment of students' hopes and dreams and serves as an inspiration to others. We appreciate and acknowledge the outstanding work of many educators who have helped to inform our scholarship and practice.

Publisher's Acknowledgments

Corwin would like to thank the following individuals for their editorial insight and guidance:

Scott Bailey
Assistant Principal
Hallsville High School
Hallsville, TX

Raylene Conner
Deputy Superintendent
Henderson Independent School District
Henderson, TX

Karen Paciotti
Assistant Professor
Texas A&M University–Corpus Christi
Corpus Christi, TX

Vance Vaughn
Assistant Professor of Educational Leadership
The University of Texas at Tyler
Tyler, TX

About the Authors

Betty J. Alford, PhD, is a professor and the chair of the Department of Secondary Education and Educational Leadership at Stephen F. Austin State University (SFASU) in Nacogdoches, Texas; serves as the doctoral program coordinator; and teaches in both the principal preparation and doctoral programs at the university. Since 1999, she has served as the lead writer for federal and state educational partnership grants totaling more than $10 million. She has served as the project director of the East Texas Gaining Early Awareness and Readiness for Undergraduate Programs (GEAR UP) grant, as the principal investigator for a second GEAR UP grant, as a co–principal investigator for a College and Career Readiness grant, as the project director for a School Leadership grant, and as the project director for Project English Language Acquisition Center of Excellence. In 2008, she received the SFASU Foundation Faculty Achievement Award for Research. Her previous awards include the department's Teaching Excellence Award and the SFASU Chapter Phi Delta Kappa Educator of the Year award. From 2004 to 2007, she served as a member of the board of the National Council of Professors of Educational Administration, and she serves as the editor of the *NCPEA Yearbook* for 2011. She holds a bachelor's degree in education from the University of Texas at Austin and a master's degree in educational supervision and counseling with certification as a school principal from SFASU. Her doctoral degree in educational administration is from the University of Texas at Austin. Her experiences in public school include service as a school principal, a school counselor, and an elementary, middle, and high school teacher.

Mary Catherine Niño, EdD, is the associate director for Project English Language Acquisition Center of Excellence, a school-university professional development partnership aimed at increasing English language learner achievement at Stephen F. Austin State University in Nacogdoches, Texas. Dr. Niño was a secondary English, social studies, and reading teacher for ten years in Texas before she entered educational leadership. She holds undergraduate and graduate degrees in English and graduate degrees in educational leadership. Realizing the need for a stronger development of content teachers' knowledge of second language acquisition processes, she worked with faculty at Stephen F. Austin State University in Nacogdoches, Texas, to foster this knowledge in preservice teacher curriculum and in professional development school sites. Responding to the changing demographics of her students, Dr. Niño developed a responsive curriculum approach that incorporated student experience, interest, language needs, and content into a cohesive approach to student learning. From this work, she has developed quality professional development for preservice and inservice teachers and principals. Dr. Niño continues to consult with area schools; model teaching in classes, working with area English as a second language coaches and teachers; and share her experiences as a content teacher integrating language development into core curriculum.

Introduction

The English language learner (ELL) student population is the fastest-growing population in the United States—at 7 times the overall national growth rate. Nationwide, ELL enrollment increased 18 percent from 2000 to 2005 (Editorial Projects in Education Research Center, 2009). Public school educational leaders were responsible for 5 million ELLs in the 2005–2006 school year, or 10 percent of the total school-aged population in the United States (National Clearinghouse for English Language Acquisition, 2010).

ELLS IN THE CURRENT EDUCATIONAL LANDSCAPE

The current political landscape and controversies surrounding immigration tend to distort educators' understanding of ELLs. For the ELL student population, which represents over 460 first languages, Spanish is the first language of 79 percent of ELLs. The Asian population, specifically Vietnamese, is second at 2 percent. While most ELLs' first language is indeed Spanish, most of them were born in the United States (Editorial Projects in Education Research Center, 2009); they are not recent immigrants. Sixty-five percent of ELLs are native-born Americans who speak a language other than English in the home. Even though the overall growth of the ELL student population throughout the nation has been 7 times higher than the rate for students in general, many educators remain ill prepared to meet the needs of ELLs. Not only do long-time educators in the field lack the knowledge and skills to teach ELLs effectively, but the trend is continuing for many recent graduates of educator preparation programs. However, a new—and growing—population of young students is entering early childhood grades with the potential for bilingualism.

The increased population of early childhood students with the potential for bilingualism is an exciting asset—not an intimidating liability. Our schools have changed and are continuing to change.

D. Short and Fitzsimmons (2007) assert that "professional development opportunities must be calibrated not to current reality, but to the changing demographics of the coming years" (p. 22). As language plays a dominant role in schooling, principals must rethink the role of language in school as they recalibrate not only to our current school demographics but also to our growing, emergent bilingual and multilingual populations. Longitudinal research shows that bilingual students outscore monolingual peers on achievement tests (Lucido & McEachern, 2000; Slavin & Cheung, 2005). Similarly, researchers (e.g., Reynolds, 1991) have shown that bilingual students also outperform monolingual peers on cognitive and metalinguistic measures. Bilingualism is clearly a cultural, professional, academic, and personal asset; however, educators sometimes perceive emergent bilinguals, or ELLs, as educational risks because there is a pedagogical gap in professional knowledge. Many teachers and leaders have not been prepared adequately to teach ELLs effectively.

A popular adage is, "All you can do is all you can do." This response issues a fitting challenge for the twenty-first century as we implement practices, processes, and policies in schools to meet the needs of ELLs. While emergent bilingualism is an exciting asset, it becomes a threatening liability when met with ill-prepared educators. To ignore the needs of ELLs is quite simply not all we can do. We can do more and are called to do more in response to real needs. When real needs are not met, the statistics presented in headlines become the reality. High failure rates, low levels of English language acquisition, and high dropout rates become the educational trajectory for the ELL population.

THE ROLE OF THE SCHOOL PRINCIPAL

This book presents the role of the school principal as a leader of learning (Leithwood, Seashore Louis, Anderson, & Wahlstrom, 2004) to strengthen practices and processes that enhance high academic achievement for all ELLs. Leithwood and Riehl (2005) identified the importance of the principal's role in setting direction, developing people, and redesigning the organization in successful campus leadership. In strengthening a positive school culture, the principal's role is critical (Deal & Peterson, 2009). The culture of a school includes the shared values, beliefs, and norms that characterize that school. School cultures can be toxic or positive, either hindering the improvement of teaching and learning or serving as a catalyst for the improvement of practice. In strengthening a school's culture to meet the needs of ELLs, a comparison of the change process and the language acquisition process yields enlightening parallels.

Parallels Between the Change Process and
Language Acquisition

Just as cultural change occurs over time and is a process rather than an event, the process of language acquisition for ELLs occurs over time. Moreover, the process of language acquisition, like the change process, does not occur in a strictly linear process. Fullan (2009) suggests that the shape of a lightning bolt is a more fitting image than a straight diagonal line for depicting the change process in schools. There may be setbacks as the school seeks to move forward, and growth may occur vividly or faintly in the process of moving forward. Likewise, Fullan's (2001) lightning metaphor versus a linear model depicts the language acquisition process. The learner may have periods of great growth, experience setbacks, and move forward again in the process of attaining mastery of another language. ELLs represent a highly diverse group with varying needs. Teachers must work to meet individual needs and recognize the uniqueness of each student. In the process of language acquisition, as in the change process, positive relationships matter.

Just as a change process includes varying phases, such as initiation, implementation, and institutionalization (Fullan, 2001), in language acquisition, there are recognized phases. Knowledge of the language processes, which are fluid and interrelated just as change processes are, can help the leader understand what to expect and how to plan interventions accordingly. Both in a change process and in assisting students in language acquisition, celebrating successes matters. Shared buy-in to the change effort is essential in achieving the goal of meeting the needs of ELLs campuswide. ELLs will engage in the life of the school throughout the day; therefore, every teacher must become a leader in fostering a school culture that promotes students' language acquisition and furthers students' learning. Ultimately, in a successful school change effort, the values, beliefs, and norms of the educators must support the change for sustained practices and processes. Ultimately, in strengthening a school culture that supports high achievement for all ELLs, shared beliefs include the benefits of a second language, an appreciation of cultural differences, and the need to overcome stereotypes and inequities. The principal is instrumental in establishing a school culture that embodies these beliefs.

ACCOUNTABILITY

With the increasing pressures of accountability performance measures and high-stakes testing based on No Child Left Behind (2001), ensuring that all students meet accountability standards is increasingly important—and expected. College and career readiness standards are also being adopted by many states nationwide (Achieve, 2009). To meet challenging academic achievement standards and guidelines for state and federal accountability measures, emphasis on rigorous content is needed for all students. Currently, the academic needs of many ELLs are not being met, which places additional pressure on schools; schools must teach both language and content to ELLs and then assess whether they have taught the content successfully—in many cases, by testing ELL students in English. In a newcomer school, for example, the principal, who had just been hired, noticed that once students were no longer exempt from the state's high-stakes assessment for language purposes, the students were returned to their home campuses although they had not mastered English. Believing that there was no true accountability to her teachers, the principal worked to change the school's policy: "We are going to keep our students, and we are going to test." Her teachers responded, "But we are going to be unacceptable."

When the fear of accountability overrides what is best for children and their attainment of both content and language, the principal must reevaluate his or her school's practice, as this principal did. This school was academically unacceptable that school year. However, this principal understood the change process and that this small step back was not an indication of failure but an indication of progress. As new programs were implemented, the school jumped to Acceptable and Recognized ratings the next year—and all subsequent years—based on the state's accountability system. This principal understood the need for an accountability system to expose achievement gaps and monitor the overall progress of her students. She did not let fear of a short-term dip in scores stop her from implementing new programs that would help her students in the long run. The principal, as leader, must show courage. This courage is founded on a conviction that doing what is right for children will inevitably show positive results.

1

Preparing for Success

Strengthening a Culture of Academic Achievement for English Language Learners

Culture has been described as "the way we do things around here" (Bennis, 1989; Deal & Peterson, 2009). A positive school culture that promotes academic achievement for English language learners (ELLs) can be seen in tangible ways, such as words of welcome written in the first language of the students, banners celebrating academic success, and inter-active learning boards reflective of cultural diversity. What we value as faculty and administrators is demonstrated by what we do. If educators value diversity of all cultures, you will see actions and artifacts to support this belief. In answering the question, Why should we focus on culture? Patricia McDonough (2008), a professor at the University of California, Los Angeles, stated, "It is the essence of a school—the values, beliefs, meanings, expectations, and assumptions that characterize the school." School cul-tures can be either toxic or productive, and the principal influences this culture to a great degree in serving as a key spokesperson for the school, as an evaluator of practices, and as a model of commitment to student success.

In this chapter, you are provided ideas for reflective practice as you consider factors that influence a school culture of academic achievement for ELLs. The chapter illuminates the principal's role in strengthening this culture by discussing four key areas: (1) building shared values, (2) build-ing positive relationships, (3) fostering conditions to promote learning, and (4) celebrating academic success (Figure 1.1).

Figure 1.1   A Culture of Academic Achievement for English Language Learners (ELLs)

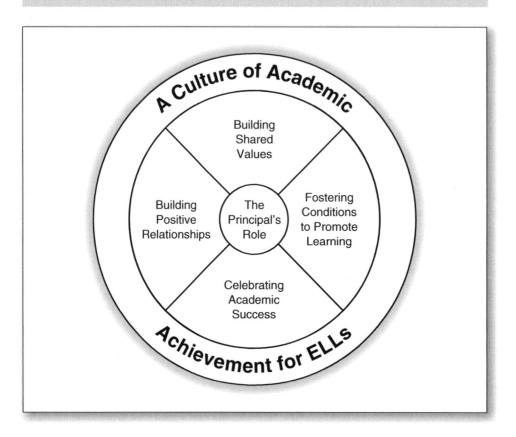

BUILDING SHARED VALUES

The principal is the school's primary communicator of the vision of high expectations for student success. By the nature of the position, the principal has multiple opportunities to serve as the school's spokesperson. Through various means, such as program introductions, articles in newsletters, morning announcements, conversations in the hallways, parent meetings, and faculty meetings, the principal has a venue for communication that can influence a culture of high expectations. As Richard Flanary (2007), senior director of the National Association of Secondary School Principals, expressed, "Establishing a school culture for student success is about moral courage. It is about using every opportunity to espouse your view and share it with parents, students, teachers, and the community" (2007).

Because a key role of the principal is to communicate the values and beliefs of the school, consider the harm of one principal's statement to a student teacher: "The ELLs are manipulative. They understand more than they let on." This extremely negative statement conveys a lack of knowledge of language acquisition as well as the principal's biased beliefs about the ELLs in his school. Contrast this message with the following statement from another principal: "When you find a barrier, go around it. Everyone deserves a quality education. My job is to find out where students are and to take them further." Or consider the actions of an elementary princi-

> **CONSIDER THIS**
>
> How often and in what manner do you communicate directly with ELLs in your school and with parents of ELLs? What are challenges to direct communication? How can these challenges be overcome?

pal who noticed blank space at the top of hall corridors and had a banner painted along the top of the hallways displaying the names of various universities as a way to plant seeds for the students' futures. Although the latter two principals were working in schools with high numbers of ELLs and a student body in which over 70 percent qualified for free and reduced lunch, these principals never stereotyped, labeled, or assumed lowered expectations for the students. Instead, these principals seized every opportunity to communicate the message of high expectations for all. They recognized the important role of teachers in reinforcing this consistent message of high expectations. As one principal emphasized, "The teacher's mindset influences student performance. The best teachers engage students and get results."

Their communication of high expectations was enhanced by positive actions, such as providing resources for college visits and materials for engaging lessons. As a principal expressed, "I give the teachers no excuses. If they need resources, we get them. We want to arm them with everything they need." Sometimes encouragement requires no additional funds, such as designating a college day with teachers wearing shirts representative of the universities they attended and encouraging positive conversations about college preparation between students and faculty. The secondary principals provided multiple opportunities for parent meetings to discuss the steps for college preparation and the importance of advanced-level secondary course selection to college preparation. They reinforced the importance of holding meetings when parents could attend. When a teacher asked why they couldn't hold the parent meetings about course selection earlier in the day, the principal quickly replied, "We can, if you don't mind parents not coming."

The principal who fosters a culture of academic achievement takes a stand for equity and excellence both in words and in actions. For example, we visited a school that had derived a vision statement of "Respect for Everyone." This theme was printed on pencils we received. Also, each grade had created a flag depicting a symbol of respect. We learned that the principal had facilitated the discussions that led to the shared vision and served as one of the key communicators of this core value of the school. The shared values were evident in the way meetings were held, decisions were made, and instruction was carried out.

BUILDING POSITIVE RELATIONSHIPS

A large part of establishing a positive culture in the school is building positive relationships with students, faculty, parents, and the community. This process involves seizing moments that can make a true difference in a student's life.

> *I asked a student who rode two metro buses to attend our charter school, "Why didn't you like your former school?" The student replied, "They were mean to us." "Why?" the principal inquired again. "Because we look funny." "You don't look funny," the principal swiftly replied. In a school with students from twenty-two countries representing sixteen native languages, students are not made to feel different. Difference is the norm, and each person's heritage is celebrated.*

ACTION POINT

Capitalize on existing community networks. Chambers of commerce exist for many cultural groups within communities. Churches offer language classes and ministries for immigrant groups. These community leaders can help get you established, offer you an introduction in a meeting, or allow you to place school information where employees or patrons clock in or enter an establishment. Being visible and establishing your presence is the first step to being rooted in the community.

A word of encouragement or a word of discouragement can be a turning point in a student's life. In the school cited above, where sixteen languages are spoken, the principal commented, "I try to learn phrases in the languages. I use a 'hooked on phonics' approach and make flash cards to say phrases such as 'Good job,' 'Good morning,' and 'Do you need help?' The students love it, and if a parent comes in who doesn't speak English, and I can say a word of welcome, the parent internalizes that we value his or her being here." The principal further shared that she is "rooted" in the community. She attends community events, and parents visit with her in the grocery store. From her five years as principal, she has developed positive relationships based on trust in an urban environment of high needs.

As principals build positive relationships with students, it is important for principals to recognize that all too often, educators assume that ELL students are at or below average instead of talented. Particularly if a student is from a low socioeconomic status family, counselors and teachers may encourage a schedule of basic courses instead of one with advanced-level courses. Consider a former ELL student who described her experience of mistakenly enrolling in an advanced physics class. Once in the class, she excelled. She pondered, "Would anyone have recognized that I was smart if this error hadn't occurred?" Or consider the comment of a college engineering student who knew no English when he enrolled in a U.S. middle school: "I had friends in high school band who were in advanced placement classes, and I said, 'I want to be in those classes.'" No one had ever encouraged him to take advanced placement classes although he was a strong student. Once in the classes, he too excelled. Contrast this lack of encouragement with the actions of school principals who meet with all students and parents to encourage participation in advanced-level courses. In short, principals can build relationships that foster student success.

FOSTERING CONDITIONS TO PROMOTE LEARNING

A vital role of the principal in strengthening a culture of academic achievement is to foster conditions that support ongoing learning (G. T. Bellamy, Fulmer, Murphy, & Muth, 2007). Conditions that support learning include hiring good teachers, providing professional development and participating as a colearner, and providing the time, space, and resources for professional development. The principal of the school where students speak sixteen languages and are learning English commented, "We look for teachers who don't mind working late." Another principal added, "You have to have the heart. The education of immigrant students has been my passion. I have a genuine interest in them and care for them. I have seen many students with many backgrounds and amazing stories. They are fighters and so courageous." In addition to heart, teachers must have knowledge and skills in content and language acquisition processes to teach ELLs effectively.

In the United States currently, four states require all preservice teachers to take specific English as a second language (ESL) coursework or to earn ESL certification (National Clearinghouse for English Language Acquisition, 2008). For many states, knowledge and skills in working with the ELL student are attained as an endorsement or specialization rather than as a requirement for all teacher education candidates. Less than one-sixth of colleges include training in working with ELLs as part of their preservice education (Menken & Antunez, 2001). Teachers enter many classrooms without the prerequisite knowledge and skills to foster achievement and educational opportunity for ELLs (Robles-Goodwin, 2006). Therefore, many practicing teachers and preservice teachers need professional development to recognize the meaning of content and language objectives and ways to meet the needs of ELLs. Professional development with coaching and follow-up is needed to assist teachers in gaining specific knowledge and skills to more effectively instruct ELLs (de Jong & Harper, 2008). In Chapter 4, we examine this process more fully.

> *Teaching is a profession, not making widgets. The best teachers are those who get results. We must stay true to our mission, and personnel are keys in achieving this. We've started lesson studies. We've participated in thirty intensive professional development institutes. I am here to help the teachers as a coach.*

Research supports that the teacher is instrumental in influencing student learning (Darling-Hammond, La Pointe, Meyerson, & Orr, 2007). One principal shared that she communicates this research while providing no excuses. Passionate about promoting a culture of academic achievement, the principal stated, "I seek to ignite the passion to make a difference for students."

In discussing those moments in teaching that demonstrate true passion in teaching, Lorraine Monroe (2000), former principal of Frederick Douglass Academy in New York, described teachable moments as moments "when true dialogue begins to transpire in class and the hairs on the back of your neck stand up acknowledging that something special is happening." Fostering true learning is the essence of education. As teachers engage students in learning, the classroom is seldom quiet; it is alive with the sounds of learning. Principals who encourage the growth of ELLs recognize the benefits of the engagement, encourage it, and celebrate it. Student engagement is not quiet work, and it is not easy work. It is, however, imperative for ELLs to put forth twice the effort as they learn academic content and language simultaneously. Without student engagement, ELLs can become passive receptacles who develop neither content nor language.

Fostering Academic Support for ELLs in a Nonremedial Manner

As mentioned previously, principals can strengthen the conditions for learning in school (G. T. Bellamy et al., 2007). They are in a unique position to influence both the times for instruction and where instruction will be provided. Principals can influence positive conditions for learning if they seize moments to do so, and when they do, they play a role in ensuring that true learning can take place. When learning is truly taking place, moments are occurring that students can recall and say, "Yes, I was there." When establishing the learning conditions for ELLs, the principal plays a key role in providing resources for quality instruction to meet students' needs. We recognize the importance of this role in considering both positive and negative experiences. Recently, a graduate student told of her principal's experiences in providing Rosetta Stone as a resource for students. When the principal asked the curriculum director about purchasing the software, he was told, "Just ask around. It's on some campus." The principal did ask and found that, indeed, the software had been purchased but only one level had been installed. When asked, the technology aid explained that the curriculum director had requested that just level 1 be installed at this time. It would be four months before the next level was installed. Immediately, the principal took the appropriate steps to have all the levels installed. He recognized his role in strengthening conditions that foster learning and immediately corrected the situation caused by the erroneous assumption that all ELLs were at the same level of instruction and would progress at the same rate. Wise principals realize that all of the many actions they take to support learning serve to strengthen a culture of academic achievement for students.

Language Development and Support Embedded in Rigorous Content

Students' native languages can be used to introduce key vocabulary. In one classroom, a teacher pretaught key vocabulary in the lesson by providing native-language translation for all seven languages represented in her classroom that period. A student noted that she had misspelled a word in his native language of Hindi. The teacher welcomed the student to the board, and he corrected it with the help of another student. Such a simple act honors and validates students' first languages and builds appreciation for all languages represented.

Principals can foster academic support by providing the resources teachers need to provide quality instruction to ELLs. At one campus for newcomers, each classroom was arranged with learning stations including a computer station, a writing station, an oral language station, and a station for direct instruction. Recognizing that not all ELLs were at the same level of instruction and would not progress at the same rate, the principal provided the scheduling, classrooms, and financial resources for teachers to differentiate for students' language proficiency levels. This wise principal realized that all of the many actions she took to support learning served to strengthen a culture of academic achievement for ELLs.

Language development and support can be embedded in rigorous content using language objectives. Many states require both a content and a language objective for all teachers—not just language or ESL teachers. Whereas a content objective often uses a verb correlating to Bloom's taxonomy (Bloom, Englehart, Furst, Hill, & Krathwohl, 1956), a language objective uses a verb that describes how a student will use language to portray how he or she understands the material learned in the content. Specifically, a language objective will use a verb that correlates with the four literacy skills: listening, speaking, reading, and writing. The content objective in a biology course may address higher-order thinking skills and ask students to evaluate a current ecological event using criteria studied in the course. The language objective in the course would then be more specific, addressing the language necessary for the student to access the content. Whereas the content objective addresses the cognitive demand, evaluation, it does not address the linguistic manner.

> **ACTION POINT**
>
> In a middle school English language arts classroom with heterogeneous proficiency levels and first languages, the teacher assigned all students identical writing assignments but designed four rubrics aligned with English proficiency levels. Expectations varied for length, grammar, and so forth but not for content or ideas (which were aligned with topics being studied). As students progressed in proficiency, language expectations changed, but content expectations remained constant. How does this meet student needs but also keep management of assessment to a minimum?

> **ACTION POINT**
>
> Tools 1.1 and 1.2 (see Chapter 6) contain tips for crafting language objectives to complement rigorous content objectives.

A more specific language objective would address the manner in which the student would evaluate through an essay, a paragraph, or an oral sentence. The language objective might also specify the academic vocabulary the student would use. The language objective would not be the same for all students. It would vary for students depending on their language proficiency level. A student with a beginning language proficiency level would retain the same content objective, but the teacher would craft an oral or visual language objective. A student with an intermediate or advanced proficiency level would retain the same content objective, but the teacher would craft an appropriate language objective— perhaps a paragraph or an essay.

Continued Support for Teachers to Achieve Scaffolded Instruction

The principal plays a key role in ensuring that all teachers obtain training in ESL methodology. As a principal explained, "Every teacher has training in ESL strategies with follow-up minitraining once a month and coaching." Another principal commented that in class walk-throughs, he gives suggestions about ways to introduce the vocabulary. The principal expressed, "I was a teacher at a school that had students from seventy-two countries who spoke forty-two different languages, and 90 percent were LEP [limited English proficiency]. I honestly believe it just takes one person to help a student meet higher goals."

Achieving scaffolded instruction, plainly put, means that while all students are working within the same content objectives, teachers provide students from different language proficiency levels different resources or parameters with which to achieve objectives. These resources and parameters change as students develop their language abilities. When we work with teachers in professional development sessions, this is sometimes a difficult concept to imagine. We show principals and teachers an image of a skyscraper being constructed. Large scaffolds are constructed alongside the skyscraper. One can see the insides of the skyscraper, the metal foundation, the wiring, the pipes, and the floors. As the skyscraper becomes solid and strong, the scaffolds are taken down. The same holds true for knowledge construction. As students' content knowledge and academic language are developed, the teacher can take away the cognitive and linguistic scaffolds provided to each student.

Not only should principals set this expectation for instruction and assessment; they should also provide support for teachers to understand and implement this level of differentiation. This approach requires an understanding of student language proficiency levels and differentiation of proficiency levels (topics discussed in Chapter 3). It also requires the principal to commit to high expectations for ELLs (a topic discussed in Chapter 2) and to provide continued support and resources for professional development and authentic scaffolded instruction. The principal who encourages a culture of academic achievement hires teachers who will engage students in learning, encourage conversation, and foster higher-level thinking skills. Supporting responsive teachers to achieve scaffolded instruction means that principals also have knowledge of second language instruction and can accurately assess appropriate linguistic modifications and accommodations within a rigorous academic context.

Increased Comprehensible Input Within Rigorous Content

From observational data in high-performing schools with large percentages of ELLs, we noted the intentional use of bulletin boards, including word walls, visuals to denote word meanings; charts of cognates; charts of explicit vocabulary words specific to the content area; and hallway displays of instructional materials as well as student work. By building connections with background knowledge for the students to aid their comprehension, the teachers promoted academic learning. The principals reinforced the importance of keeping the content high while also increasing comprehensible input. As one principal stated, "Five years ago when I first came to this school, there was a lot of coloring. Also, teachers would tell students to look up words in the dictionary whenever they didn't understand. This wasted a great deal of instructional time. I told them, 'Unless you are teaching dictionary skills, don't send the student to the dictionary for every unknown word.'" Teachers made content comprehensible by providing visuals, capitalizing on ELLs' background knowledge, preteaching academic vocabulary, strategically using native languages, and scaffolding instruction. Because principals and teachers were able to provide comprehensible input to the students without watering down the curriculum, they provided equitable access to rigorous content.

Facilitating Collaborative Relationships During the School Day

The principal can encourage time for professional development and resources to enhance learning and can foster collaboration for joint planning to meet students' needs. One principal stressed, "It's important that everyone feels ownership and believes that 'these are our students.' We want teachers to truly believe that 'this is our school.'" With shared ownership through team planning, professional development, and follow-up coaching, teachers can strengthen skills in meeting the needs of ELLs. Another principal described how she works with teachers: "I work with grade-level chairs. We discuss the bilingual needs and the English needs. I ask the physical education teacher to share how [she is] supporting the content teachers. It is our belief that if perpendicular lines are taught in math, they should also be taught in art. We try to integrate our content areas. We are trying to be more vertically aligned. I constantly stress that times have changed. We must model, tell, and demonstrate. In a school with 25 percent LEP [limited English proficiency] students, we're constantly providing help for the content teachers in all classes."

The principals did not merely manage the time to collaborate and develop professionally; instead, the principals worked alongside the teachers, modeling the vision for success and expectations for students and collaborating with the professional community.

Providing Support

Principals can seek resources for their students and opportunities for support. Consider the principal who visited with his school's valedictorian, who was waiting tables as his part-time job in college. The principal quickly offered the young man a job as a tutor at his school, stating, "I can give you a much better job than this while you are in college. Come see me tomorrow." He hired the young man as a tutor for students and worked around the young man's college schedule. In this community of immigrants, the principal recognized the strong value of building positive relationships, encouraging high achievement, and providing support for success. Another urban principal commented, "We employ college tutors in all of our Algebra I and geometry classes and most biology and integrated and physical science classes." This principal's actions mirror his stated belief that each student "deserves a quality education. My job is to find out where students are and take them further."

CELEBRATING ACADEMIC SUCCESS

In their book *Shaping School Culture,* Deal and Peterson (2009) emphasize the importance of celebrations as a reinforcement of what the school values. In achieving a culture of academic achievement, academic success is celebrated. Celebrations of academic success can be noted through tangible artifacts, programs, or announcements, but the celebration of student learning can also occur simply through an encouraging word. One principal shared, "What does it cost to smile and say 'good morning'?" Principals can celebrate academic success in multiple ways. The stories of success that are shared and the role models that are provided are additional ways that principals can celebrate academic success and encourage a culture of academic achievement for all. As the U.S. assistant secretary for the Office of Elementary and Secondary Education Thelma Melendez (2010b) stated in her conference presentation at the College Board Prepárate, "Students need to hear, 'I believe in you, and you can achieve great things.'"

> I don't know of anyone who celebrates more than we do. Every six weeks, we have an assembly, and we give medals for multiple areas, such as improvement, school behavior, and academic excellence. The medals are displayed outside the team area, and the team that receives the greatest number of medals also keeps the four-foot trophy or display. After we received the rating of Exemplary through our state's accountability system, each student, cafeteria worker, administrator, custodian, parent volunteer, and teacher was provided a T-shirt celebrating our success. We had a steak dinner for teachers, and teachers were provided a half day as a personal day while community volunteers staffed our classrooms. We also had a celebration for our students.

sounds great

Today's school leaders are facing an intricate world with new challenges and complex barriers that must be overcome if they are to create learning environments in which all students can succeed (Schlechty, 2008). Leadership is needed to transform schools to meet these challenges (Reyes & Wagstaff, 2005) and to turn schools into arenas of learning for all (Leithwood & Riehl, 2005). This chapter contributes to the understanding of practices and processes of principal leadership that strengthen academic achievement and educational opportunity for ELLs and move campuses toward systemic, whole-campus reform to meet the needs of ELLs. This illumination of key practices and processes in principal leadership can be used to guide reform efforts in schools as principals create these conditions, reform current contexts of inequity, and turn their direct attention to the needs of ELLs—needs that are of the utmost importance in today's world.

CASE STUDY

In a school-university partnership, principals were the catalysts in making the vision of high expectations possible through practical implementation. The principals who provided structures for collaboration experienced higher levels of implementation on their campuses. The following case examines the actions taken by secondary principals to ensure the implementation of high expectations for ELLs, best practices for comprehensible input, and a coaching model.

A Structure of Collaboration

Structures for collaboration between teachers, between teachers and coaches, and between coaches and university faculty were necessary for the change effort to be effected at the classroom level. Access to resources and networking was required before significant changes were accomplished at the classroom instructional level. This structure was largely due to the level of instructional leader support on each campus.

Instructional Leader Support

Principals on the secondary campuses garnered support from teachers by attending university trainings alongside coaches and teachers, being present in on-campus trainings, and following up with teachers and coaches on lessons learned during professional development. Principals incorporated language objectives, scaffolding, and strategies for increasing comprehensible input into observational expectations. In addition, principals arranged for coaches' classes to be covered when they were observing other teachers or working collaboratively during planning periods. Above all, principals' high expectations for teachers to deliver quality content to ELLs were critical to the success of the change effort. As one participant noted, teachers are "a little leery at first when it's all thrown at them." Principals not only had high expectations for teachers but also provided support in concert with the professional development project to realize the expectations. The critical link for effective implementation of rigor and support at the classroom level was the campus instructional leader's level of support for facilitating structures of collaboration.

On Campuses

The culture of collaboration fostered positive attitudes toward moving educators to high expectations for all students and equitable access to rigorous curriculum for ELLs. Rather than laying blame on teachers, engaging in critical dialogue fostered further discussions designed to address the critical issues. Facilitating dialogue to achieve transformation rather than stagnant complaining required structuring professional development around a process of dialogic engagement. This process began with a coaches' training using Lindsey, Martinez, and Lindsey's (2007) approach to reflective conversations and problem-solving conversations. Coaches had previously indicated concerns about engaging teachers in critical conversations or attempting to move campus cultures to include rigor and high expectations for all learners. Training in the process of coaching through conversation and seizing the "opportunity to shift thinking" (Lindsey et al., 2007, p. 152) in a nonconfrontational, collaborative, and supportive manner was a critical step in moving coaches to facilitating collaboration effectively on their campuses at the classroom level.

> *I meet with my teachers on the second and fourth week of every month. We have a curriculum meeting, and different topics are initiated. I've also surveyed the teachers to find out which professional development topics they are wanting. By their conversations, I also learn of needs. For example, I write a newsletter. Last week's topic was "These Kids Don't Speak English? What Do I Do?" I pulled some different web articles and sites the teachers could go to in order to help them to understand second language learners. At the beginning of the year, we also talked about the development of language acquisition and the myth of "This child is just really, really shy. He or she never says a word." Understanding that this silent period is actually a stage of language acquisition is important. This is a natural progression. Yet during the first weeks of school, teachers were screaming, "Really, they don't speak? They don't talk? They don't understand me?" In response, we've continued talking about how we can best support students. We opened one of our professional development sessions with a discussion question: "What do high expectations look like?" Some of the teachers gave excuses, such as "This child is a second language learner, so I can't have the same high expectations." I asked the challenging question, "Wouldn't you have the same expectations that the child should be able to compete with his or her same-aged peers?" I think discussions—those hard ones about race, about culture, and about differences—are important. That is capacity building in the knowledge base and making it part of who we are. As we continue to dialogue about curriculum, about instruction, and about strategies, I've started to hear the buzz in the teachers' lounge. That's how I know we're making changes. The conversation is "Did you try this strategy?" or "I did this and it worked," or "We've had this article about working with ELLs. Did you get a chance to read it?" I put articles in their boxes, not as forced reading, and they are reading them. Instead of having faculty meetings this year, we have had vertical team meetings, and the teams are talking about strategies that are effective with the ELLs.*

Curricular Collaboration

Teachers began working to contextualize knowledge for ELLs so that moving from one subject to the next was a natural transition. In addition, research supports organizing curriculum for ELLs around big questions or themes (Freeman & Freeman, 2007) to increase comprehensible input and make content more contextual. The collaboration between the curricular objectives requires collaboration between teachers for implementation. Participants indicated that a structure within the curriculum has helped increase collaboration between teachers. Teachers have also worked to provide curricular collaboration as they have integrated language and literacy objectives into each content area. This collaboration provided common language for teachers to plan, instruct, and assess literacy skills, and it strengthened consistency for students as they worked in content areas to develop literacy skills. Through this process, a culture of academic achievement for ELLs has been strengthened.

> *I think that the ELL teaching strategies are very good teaching strategies. I let the teachers know that this isn't an add-on or something that's effective just for ELLs. Attending these professional development opportunities will really make your teaching better, and the strategies that you will learn will benefit all your students. I think we must provide teachers the opportunity to grow professionally and to be able to use as many strategies as they can. We talk about "What are we going to do to enhance learning for the ELLs? Are we challenging the students?" We look at our achievement data and talk about ways we can more fully meet students' needs. I'm not going to prescribe something for the teachers. They're the ones with the special expertise.*

QUESTIONS TO CONSIDER

1. In which ways did the principals build shared values and structures for collaboration?

2. How did their practices and processes strengthen the culture of high expectations?

3. What are the critical roles of the principal in strengthening a culture of high expectations?

2

Advocating for Student Success

Many schools are in need of reform to meet the needs of English language learners (ELLs) through a schoolwide commitment to increased academic achievement (Gandara & Contreras, 2009). Although the past decade has been characterized by school reform, declarations of the failure of many large-scale reform efforts have also emerged (Cuban, Lichtenstein, Evenchik, Tombari, & Pozzoboni, 2010). In one study of school reform, Cuban et al. (2010) identify the cause of such failures as an emphasis on structural rather than instructional changes. The good news is that some schools have focused on instructional changes to better meet the needs of ELLs and to advocate for student success. The result has been school improvement. For example, for school campuses with high percentages of ELLs who have received Exemplary recognition on the state's accountability system measures, the campuses shared the following characteristics. All teachers are English as a second language (ESL) certified and use ESL strategies to engage their students and to monitor results. The principals understand the importance of meeting each student's needs and communicate this positive message to parents, students, community members, and faculty. Furthermore, the principals serve as advocates for all students' academic success.

THE ROLE OF RECULTURING IN ADVOCACY

Listed among the many R words associated with the reforms of the past decade, such as *revitalizing, reengineering, refreshing, rethinking, renewing,* and *redesigning,* reculturing has been a consistent characteristic of successful school reforms. As we discussed in Chapter 1, shaping the culture of the school into a culture of high expectations implies that the values, beliefs, norms, policies, processes, and practices of the individuals in the school are aligned with a consistent vision. The principal assists in navigating the "complex interaction of organizational, structural, instructional, and staffing issues behind the achievement of English learners" (Horowitz et al., 2009, p. iv). In a study of four urban districts (Dallas, New York City, San Francisco, and St. Paul) that achieved substantial gains for ELLs on academic measures, researchers found, "In each of the improving districts, there was a particularly effective, vocal advocate for the improvement of ELL instruction and services who was skillful in forming strategic partnerships and rallying support behind their reform agendas" (Horowitz et al., 2009, p. 2). In shaping improved academic performance, it was important that the reform was based on clear needs that were communicated clearly and received broad-based acknowledgment that action was needed (Horowitz et al., 2009). The principal can be instrumental in this process.

In this chapter, we discuss the importance of building a shared understanding of needs through data analysis, the importance of authenticity and commitment in building relationships as an advocate for students, and the importance of establishing structures to support key principles and high-yield instructional practices for ELLs. Each of these elements provides opportunities for the school principal to advocate for increased student academic success.

BUILDING A SHARED UNDERSTANDING OF NEEDS THROUGH DATA ANALYSIS

Moving from pockets of excellence in individual classrooms to a schoolwide culture of high expectations presents a challenge to schools that are seeking to achieve academic excellence and bridge the achievement gap for ELLs (Elmore, 2005). To achieve this type of reform, the principal leads the way in helping school personnel learn to recognize and assess national, state, and local ELL needs through the analysis of relevant data. Chubb and Loveless (2002) emphasize the urgency of overcoming the achievement gap as follows: "Overstating the importance of the achievement gap is not easy. The difference in educational achievement between White students, on the one hand, and African and Hispanic students, on the other, is large and persistent. In the last decade, it's gotten worse" (p. 1).

In addition, according to 2006–2007 National Assessment of Educational Progress (NAEP) data, as compiled by Editorial Projects in Education Research Center (EPE, 2009), 25 percent of ELLs in the United States did not make progress toward proficiency in English, which only exacerbates the issue of academic proficiency and further widens the academic achievement gap. Also, according to NAEP data as reported by EPE (2009), ELL academic achievement is improving, but a significant gap remains between ELLs and all other students. On 2007 NAEP scores, a 25.2 percent achievement gap in math still exists as does a 24.8 percent gap in reading. A comparison of ELL performance on state-developed assessments revealed similar achievement gaps, with a 23.6 percent achievement gap in math and a 32.3 percent achievement gap in reading (EPE, 2009).

Graduation rates, another external indicator of academic achievement, indicate that 64 percent of ELLs graduated from high school in 2006 in the United States; however, this figure varies widely from state to state, ranging from less than 40 percent in Georgia to over 85 percent in Hawaii (EPE, 2009). The percentage also varies greatly by ethnicity and the manner in which states calculate graduation rates (EPE, 2010). Nonetheless, the numbers still indicate a 16 percent gap between ELLs and all other students. The graduation rate of Hispanic students—the largest group represented in the ELL demographic—was 55.5 percent in 2006 compared to 76.6 percent for white students. Again, while these data have the potential to paint a grim picture, a leader working to advocate for ELLs uses data to communicate the need for change and to develop a sense of urgency among faculty.

Conyers and Ewy (2004) emphasize that "the challenge of teaching all students and closing the gap in student achievement will not go away" (p. 2). Leadership is needed to meet this challenge. In the report titled "Succeeding With English Language Learners" (Horowitz et al., 2009), the authors indicate that data use was a "cornerstone of their reform strategies, significantly expanding the accessibility, quantity, and types of student data available to educators" (p. 3), while "instructional needs of ELLs appeared to have been an afterthought" in schools where ELLs were underperforming (p. 30).

In leading the analysis of student data, the principal must recognize that data reflect real people. Educators' actions and words can be a roadblock for the ELLs' future or a catalyst for positive next steps. In speaking to a group of educators, the U.S. assistant secretary for the Office of Elementary and Secondary Education, Dr. Thelma Melendez (2010a), shared the following. (Dr. Melendez was the recipient of the Superintendent of the Year award for California while at Pomona Independent School District [ISD] and currently serves as assistant secretary for the Office of Elementary and Secondary Education for the U.S. Department of Education.) In the vignette, note the difference in the two educators' responses of "Absolutely not" and "Absolutely."

I feel blessed to have had a career serving children in public education. In each position I've held—whether as a teacher, principal, superintendent, or now, as an Assistant Secretary—my guiding principle has been the same. I am focused on what will improve teaching and learning to help ensure the success of all our children. For me this is more than a moral argument, or a sound professional philosophy—it is rooted in the events of my own life. I went to kindergarten at Fremont Elementary School in Montebello, California—right near Los Angeles. I am the daughter of Mexican immigrants, and we spoke Spanish, my first language, at home. I remember my first day of school wasn't easy. It was difficult to communicate with my classmates and my teacher. But one teacher, Mrs. Silverman, didn't see this as a problem. She saw it as an opportunity. She took it upon herself to find a way to teach me. Mrs. Silverman always made sure I knew what was happening in class, giving me attention and encouragement whenever I needed extra help. From that first day, Mrs. Silverman believed that I could succeed and took steps to make sure I did. So I know what it means to benefit from high expectations. But I also know how hard it is overcome low expectations. When I was in high school, I went to meet with my guidance counselor. I asked her if she thought I should apply to UCLA. "No way. Absolutely not," she said. She had not even looked at the file on her desk with my SAT scores and grades. All she knew about me was my last name. She assumed community college was perfect for me. Now two-year schools are fine places, but that was not my dream. My dream was to attend UCLA. Consequently, it would take me longer to get there. I began at a Cal State school. But there, once again I was fortunate to have a teacher who had high expectations of me. One day, after a long test, I visited my political science professor. He taught at both the Cal State and at UCLA. So I repeated the question I posed two years earlier: Could I make it at UCLA? His answer was as quick and as definitive as my guidance counselor's—except shorter. "Absolutely," he said. And he was right. UCLA accepted me based on the same high school grades and college admissions scores that sat unopened on my guidance counselor's desk. I did graduate from UCLA, and went on to earn my doctorate at USC. Experience has taught me that education equalizes differences in background, culture and privilege, and gives every child a fair chance. My story speaks to the importance of high expectations, great teaching, and access to and success in higher education. My story also speaks to the dangers of low expectations, uninspired teaching, and inequitable access—especially for historically underserved groups.

Sadly, the dangers in my story are the reality of too many of our school children today. Where I was able to rise, today, too many don't. I am honored and passionate about working on their behalf, and helping to ensure their success. It's the best way I know of to repay Mrs. Silverman and all the others like her who helped me, and to carry on the noblest traditions of the teaching profession. It's also, quite simply, the right thing to do.

DATA ANALYSIS

Data analysis is highly important in foster-ing school improvement and alleviating the achievement gap (Herman, Aschbacher, & Winters, 1992). In the current context of the No Child Left Behind legislation, states across the nation have instituted testing based on standards, and administrators, legislators, and communities compare school performance. For example, in Texas, the State Accountability System is based on the Texas Essential Knowledge and Skills curriculum framework, with students tested on the Texas Essential Knowledge and Skills through the Texas Assessment of Academic Skills. However, it is important for the prin-cipal to lead the staff beyond one single measure of performance to a multitude of performance measures that serve as indicators of the school's success in increasing the performance of students and bridging the achievement gap. Specifically, the principal can lead the faculty in understanding the diversity of ELLs in the school by looking at the available data. Diversity is represented in multiple ways, such as income level, length of time in the United States, and proficiency in English. In addition, the ESL director can provide or work with the teachers to create a profile of the students, which could include educa-tional background, prior experiences, refugee status, cultural background, and language distance (Fairbairn & Jones-Vo, 2010). These profiles paint a more holistic view of each ELL student and help teachers gain valuable insight into each student's educational experience.

> **CONSIDER THIS**
>
> *Language distance* is a term used to describe how different languages are from one another. The more linguistically different a language is from English, the more difficult it is to learn. Consider the data of your school and the home languages represented. Why are these data additional relevant pieces to add to the profile? How can the principal use the data responsibly to help teachers understand their students?

> *It's one thing to collect the data, particularly what the public receives, but if that is all administrators are concentrating on, then they are shortchanging the public. The administrators need to be able to see beyond the TAKS [Texas Assessment of Academic Skills] test to consider, "Where does the campus stand with the other data concerning the school?" Look at who is 50 percent, who is 40 percent and below. Analyze the data appropriately to present them to the public. Analyze what are good and what are bad data and which are statistically significant. Ask, "Are we getting better?" We want all our students achieving to high levels, but as administrators, we need to know when we see an anomaly. We need to be able to analyze the data appropriately.*

Educators should also consider state and national demographic trends that affect the school. Results on accountability measures, such as state assessments, local benchmark tests, dual-credit and advanced placement (AP) course participation and success, and college entrance examinations, can be disaggregated by ethnic group to discern gaps in achievement, and plans of action can then be formulated. For example, in our geographical area, data pointed to the need both to revise the teacher education program and to provide professional development for current teachers. Results of a survey indicated that although teachers valued cultural diversity, they didn't know what to do to assist ELLs with content in English. Demographic projections indicated that teachers would continue to need these strategies. Analyzing data resulted in a partnership to provide professional development and revise the teacher education program to meet ELLs' needs. In summary, principals must guide the faculty in taking a holistic approach to data analysis, viewing educational reform as a continuous improvement process (Fullan, 2001).

School improvement processes that emphasize the involvement of all stakeholders and strengthen relationships are essential to successful school leadership (Donaldson, 2008; Duffy, 2004). Through studying the accountability data and truly understanding the school through equity audits, a critical mass can develop that shares an understanding of the needs that are driving the reform to a schoolwide emphasis on ELL achievement.

> *I think organizational and communication skills are most important, especially how to lead to a culture of high performance. The ideas about and resources for how to do that are important to share. Top to bottom works with only a very few individuals. Instead, principals need to develop a system to give voice from the bottom to the top, letting all assist in the knowledge sharing. If all are on the same page, it helps to build the culture.*

BUILDING RELATIONSHIPS AS AN ADVOCATE FOR STUDENTS

THE IMPORTANCE OF AUTHENTICITY AND COMMITMENT

Authenticity and commitment to the core principles of the school are demonstrated in the principal's actions and words on behalf of teachers, parents, and students. As an elementary principal commented, "I have heard that the ELL parents don't feel valued by the teachers at a neighboring school. That would not happen here. We will help all parents to feel welcome at our school." This firm commitment in words is followed by actions, such as hiring bilingual teachers, enlisting additional translators for report card nights, and forming a solid parent-school compact. Advocating for change in policies and practices to better meet the needs of ELLs is demonstrated in words and actions, but if the words are not sincere and the commitment to all students achieving at high levels is not genuine, the changes will not be long term. As discussed in Chapter 1, to effect a shift to a stronger culture of high expectations, a genuine commitment to the goal must be demonstrated. Very quickly, faculty, students, and parents recognize when words are not parallel with actions. They recognize what is real.

I have often thought about an incident that occurred while I was visiting a campus where I had served as principal the previous year. I had moved to a new city, but I stopped by the school to leave some materials. As I walked down the sidewalk, a young girl ran up excitedly, hugged me, and said, "A real principal." I'll never forget that moment. I have often wondered, "What caused this choice of words? Was it my dress? Was it my demeanor?" I hope it was that she felt a connectedness between my words and actions, that she felt valued, that she felt supported, that she felt I genuinely cared.

> *If I heard that teachers were saying, "The parents just don't care," I'd be meeting with these teachers to make a plan for improvement, or they would not be on my campus. In a school with 68 percent Latino students and many parents who do not speak English, we have found that hiring many interpreters to help with report night is essential. We now provide all report cards through personal conferences between the student, the teacher, and the parent. We have been highly successful. Our Parent Teacher Association has also changed in membership through the past three years. At one time, our teachers dominated the officer positions. Now, the officers are all parents. We've offered a literacy program for our non-English-speaking parents to strengthen ways for them to work with their children at home on reading skills. Parents want to be involved with their children's education. They may not know how.*

At a favorite coffee shop, I read a sign each day promoting "real food." I generally smile and think, "Is there unreal food?" Although the phrase makes me smile, I know what the business is attempting to convey. Just as we recognize the beauty of a real diamond or the nourishment of real food, we recognize the congruity between words and actions. We recognize when the principal authentically cares and backs up that commitment with positive actions.

Starratt (2004) stresses the importance of authentic leadership in which the leader views his or her role as a moral responsibility that embodies characteristics of mutual respect and support. Meaningful relationships can be built on an understanding of *confianza*—a combination of trust, mutual respect, comfort, familiarity, and understanding based on positive relationships. Establishing this trust is important and is strengthened as authentic school leaders model the philosophy of equity and excellence and foster the mindset of high expectations for all. Donaldson (2006) describes trust as the glue that holds the organization together and propels it forward to excellence. As an administrator said, "It is important to know who you are and your own personal philosophy and what your own personal philosophy is based upon." Another administrator emphasized that "it is easy to tell when an educator is just saying the words. These aren't the persons we need leading our schools." Yet another administrator stressed to a college professor of educational administration, "Teach them to be advocates for students. If we don't advocate for the students, who will?" These administrators expressed a sense of urgency in bridging the achievement gap and promoting high expectations from all educators while establishing positive relationships built on trust.

ESTABLISHING STRUCTURES TO SUPPORT KEY PRINCIPLES AND HIGH-YIELD INSTRUCTIONAL PRACTICES FOR ELLS

In strengthening a culture of high expectations for all students, ongoing communication is important. Outreach will be provided to all stakeholders, structures of collaboration will be designed, and crucial conversations will occur on issues of social justice. The communication is ongoing, and a clear focus on meeting the needs is present. Collaborative structures of monthly school-based team meetings, weekly teacher team meetings, and monthly parent advisory meetings provide opportunities for data analysis and ongoing improvement planning. The principal provides leadership through establishing structures to ensure that meaningful dialogue can occur with multiple stakeholders.

Schools have been criticized for not studying best practices and learning from one another (Fullan, 2005). Ongoing learning and acquiring specific knowledge of recommended curriculum practices in various fields are highly important. As an administrator commented, "I once thought that all that I needed to know was what good pedagogy looked like. Now, I realize that I need to know what is recommended as best practice in teaching math, English, history, etc. I must stay abreast of curriculum reform."

The principal serves as an advocate of student learning through reinforcement of important guiding principles and instructional strategies in teaching ELLs. The principal engages the faculty in discussing the principles that will inform their actions. Examples of principles and resulting actions are provided, but they do not constitute an exhaustive list by any means. This list is provided not as a blueprint. Rather, it is hoped that the list will lead to brainstorming and implementation of additional promising practices in support of principles to guide educators' work.

- *A schoolwide literacy focus is important.* In recognition of this principle, the principal ensures that a print-rich environment is fostered. The ESL director serves as a resource for content teachers and is an integral part of the school improvement team. Ways to encourage vocabulary development are fostered.
- *The student should be encouraged to maintain his or her first language.* Recognizing the vital importance of learning English as the gateway to academic success, the principal also honors the student's first language and recognizes the benefits of bilingualism.
- *Diversity is a strength on which to build.* The principal models an appreciation for cultural differences. Cultural fairs and extracurricular activities that meet the interests of diverse students are evident.
- *It is important to get to know the students, including their likes and dislikes, their goals, and their families.* The principal knows students' names. He or she elicits students' views through surveys, open discussion, and student advisory groups. He or she establishes structures for interaction in small settings through advisory periods and mentoring programs.
- *Building positive relationships matters.* The principal takes the time to listen to students, to build trust, and to create shared understanding. The principal is approachable, models an ethic of care, and is a visible presence at community events as well as students' cocurricular or extracurricular activities.
- *The initial problem may not be the problem.* The principal encourages in-depth problem solving. For example, lack of parental interest in a child's education is sometimes identified as the problem. Instead, other factors may be the challenges to address, such as transportation needs, child care needs, and the times of meetings.
- *Communication through websites and newsletters in the predominant languages spoken by students is helpful as a resource to parents and students.* In Houston ISD, for example, three languages are predominant in the district. On the website, a publication titled "How Can We Help You?" is written in the three languages.
- *Afterschool clubs or tutoring, before-school tutoring, and summer programs can be highly beneficial.* Providing afterschool language-intensive instruction with transportation afterward is but one possibility for enhancing learning opportunities.
- *Cognizant of the home language surveys and the number of parents or guardians who do not speak English, hiring interpreters as well as bilingual teachers and aides is important.* The principal identifies the need for interpreters in consultation with the ESL director.
- *Seeking community resources to assist in meeting ELLs' learning needs is highly beneficial.* The principal serves as an integral part of the community and seeks community members as school resources. For example, in Ysleta ISD, a grandmother who speaks only Spanish

serves as a guest speaker in schools and tells the children stories of her life as a young girl. In Houston ISD, an author speaks to the ELL students about the steps of writing and engages them in writing activities.

- *Requiring all teachers to attain ESL certification is important.* Providing ongoing follow-up and support through coaching, monthly meetings, and other professional development opportunities is equally important.

- *Leveraging resources is an important principal leadership role in strengthening a culture of high achievement for ELLs.* The principal works with the ESL director in the administration of Title III funds to discern ways that a schoolwide focus on meeting ELL needs can be achieved. Securing grants, using discretionary funds effectively, and enlisting community support are all important practices and processes for leveraging resources to implement a plan to meet the needs of ELLs.

- *Rigor is important.* The principal monitors classroom instruction and ensures that students are engaged and challenged by the work that is assigned. As one principal shared, "the first year I was principal, when I went into the ELL classrooms, I saw a lot of coloring." Gandara (2008) stresses, "A command of academic English must be explicitly taught; it does not occur naturally" (p. 75).

- *Successful school reform does not occur without quality professional development.* In influencing the school culture, professional development is characterized by dialogue and discussion of values and beliefs to support the reform.

- *Distributed leadership is important in successful school leadership.* As Collins (2001) identifies in the book *Good to Great,* "The right people are in the right seats" (p. 41). These individuals influence positive actions that are implemented with ongoing evaluation, celebration of successes, and refinements in a continuous improvement cycle. Flexibility is provided to meet the needs of the local context.

The Principal's Role

By nature of the principal's role as the primary administrator of the school, the principal has many opportunities to reinforce these guiding principles. Serving as an advocate for student learning is not a passive event. Advocacy implies actions and collaborative decision making. In the classroom, there are many instructional strategies that are helpful to the ELL. The principal can encourage these strategies, facilitate peer coaching for modeling strategies, and provide staff development to help teachers acquire the knowledge as well as monitor and reinforce the strategies. These instructional strategies include, but are not limited to, the following:

- using visuals, graphs, Venn diagrams, and models;
- providing extra time for writing in a second language;

- planning for student engagement;
- requiring students to keep a vocabulary journal;
- teaching language phrases that may be difficult;
- teaching multiple meanings of words;
- teaching words with similar meanings;
- providing explicit instruction on high-frequency words;
- providing explicit instruction on content-specific keywords;
- building background knowledge of a concept;
- providing books and resources to build skills in listening, speaking, reading, and writing;
- using sentence starters such as "What I like is...";
- providing safe ways to practice English;
- providing multiple opportunities to engage in discussion; and
- monitoring improvement.

Principals serve as instructional leaders by recognizing best practices and serving as advocates for the implementation of these practices. They participate in the school's ongoing professional development efforts to better meet the needs of ELLs, obtaining ongoing professional development through varied formats (e.g., peer coaching, site visits, and book studies), rather than seeking the one-shot professional development experiences that once dominated our profession. Recommendations of the National Staff Development Council of quality professional development can be used as a guide for ensuring quality professional development experiences for teachers of ELLs. For professional development and implementation of school improvement processes, leveraging resources is also important.

Leithwood and Riehl (2005) asserted that the principal is key in setting direction, developing people, and redesigning the organization. In successful partnerships, key individuals serve as champions of the cause by maintaining a clear focus on meeting identified needs. There are few shortcuts to success. Although collaboration, professional development, and communication are important processes in achieving the goal of increased student learning, leadership to support and guide the process is essential.

The leader responds to the urgent need to raise student achievement through academic rigor and relevance for all students and serves as an advocate for student learning. The need to assist all students in receiving a high-quality education to ensure both equity and excellence and to bridge the current achievement gap is critical. Gandara (2008) reports, "Although completion rates of some ethnic groups is improving, Latino students—from whom the majority of immigrant students and English learners are drawn—appear to be making little progress toward earning college degrees. Many recent reform proposals have focused on the need to strengthen the pipeline to college for these students, without discernible positive outcomes" (p. 72).

Ensuring that ELLs aren't placed in the pipeline of less rigorous courses requires outreach. Latino students make up the largest ethnic group of ELLs. However, they are underrepresented both in the numbers sitting for AP tests and in those receiving college credit (College Board, 2006). As students gain command of the English language, principals can help ensure that the students are prepared for college and careers. Adelman (1999), while senior policy analyst for the U.S. Department of Education, reported that a student's course-taking pattern is the most important indicator of success in college and is more important than grade point average or class rank.

CASE STUDY

While English proficiency, native language maintenance, and bicultural-ism are key areas of concern for ELLs, as advocates for ELLs, principals should focus a widened lens on increased participation in rigorous courses, college-going readiness, and longitudinal academic success. English proficiency is not an end; it is one step on the same educational journey all students take. Principals should not view ELLs as finished products when they have attained English proficiency; rather, instruc-tional leaders should have similar expectations of career and college readiness for ELLs as those they would have for all students.

In the following case study, key practices and processes for increasing student participation and success in advanced-level courses are shared. The results of the case study include exam-ples of the instructional leader's actions as an advocate for all learners in removing barriers to participation in AP courses, in providing high-quality professional devel-opment, in implementing strategies for school improvement with outreach and support, and in strengthening teacher buy-in to the change.

> **CONSIDER THIS**
>
> Analyze the key administrative practices that these instructional leaders engaged in and consider ways that they served as advocates for students.

Removal of Barriers

Removal of barriers to participation in more rigorous classes was a key administrative practice in increasing student participation in advanced-level courses. The firm commitment of principals to each student's success was evident when they discussed the criteria of placement for advanced classes. Consider the following quotes:

- "Never say, 'Absolutely not!' If we fault, we want to fault on the side of the students [being given a chance to take the more rigorous classes]. It's a mindset in many ways."

- "People have preconceived ideas of an AP student. I ask teachers to define 'What is an AP student?' There's no mold. If we had said, 'Is Hernandez [who gained 41 college hours through AP] an AP student?' we would have said, 'No.' He was from a very poor family. That's the mindset you need to break. There's no mold for an AP student."

The two quotations above illustrate a passionate commitment to not closing opportunities for students. This commitment was common among the voices of administrators who were successful in sustaining the change toward inclusive policies and practices for admission to secondary advanced-level courses.

> *I have a vision. What I want is a choice for all students. At graduation, a student could go left into an institution of higher learning or right to get a skilled job. Each could cross and go either way because they all have taken college-level courses.*

The demands of our twenty-first century are requiring an emphasis on advanced-level courses. The principals were cognizant of their role as enforcers of inclusive policies and practices for rigorous courses and were willing to take a stand for all students. Principals paid explicit attention to traditionally tracked students, such as those currently and formerly labeled limited English proficient, to ensure that all students benefited from the rigor of an advanced curriculum.

> *We feel that students should take the AP classes. These classes provide exposure to quality teaching. Whether the student passes the AP test or not, the student benefits. The instruction is important, not just whether the student passes the test. Some of the teachers still want to restrict access to students. Until we get out of the mindset that our role is to educate the top one-third and forget the rest, there's a problem.*

Leaders must be willing to take a stand, recognizing that school leadership is a moral endeavor (Sergiovanni, 2007; Starratt, 2004). In short, these principals cared and were willing to take a stand in promoting and enforcing inclusionary practices for advanced-level courses. The principals modeled the philosophy that we must do everything possible to persuade students to stay in the more rigorous college-level classes. Inclusionary practices included an expectation that teachers provide students the resources for success—from extra help and tutoring to additional scaffolds and knowledge to fill in learning gaps. Only if the student could not pass after extended effort on the part of the leader, educator, and student would a transfer to a regular class be allowed. As one principal emphasized, "It is now as hard to get out of an advanced-level class as it used to be to get in, and the regular-level classes are also being taught to a challenging level."

STRATEGIES FOR SCHOOL IMPROVEMENT AND STUDENT OUTREACH AND SUPPORT

To avoid the tracking of students, AP classes were open to all students. However, the principals were quick to stress that the AP program serves as a driving force for the curriculum. They stated that in some districts, the state's minimum competency testing program is "driving the curriculum and is the focus of the school." These administrators all expressed that the schools had moved beyond just an emphasis on the state's minimum competency test as the main emphasis of the school. As an administrator emphasized, "The AP program is the backbone of our focus." In their roles as communicators of the benefits of the program, administrators were quick to suggest that the benefits of participation in the AP program are present even if students do not pass the AP exam.

> *In our district there used to be a saying, "Back by Halloween," because the students who went away to college had already failed by Halloween. Now, students are better prepared to go to college and are successful there.*

All of the administrators communicated that they invite former students to come back to talk to students about the benefits of taking the harder classes. As an administrator stressed, "Having our former students come back is most powerful." This student outreach helps emphasize and reinforce the college-going culture of the whole school. This personalized support extends to recruiting students for the harder classes as well. The recruitment process includes meetings with parents, information in newsletters, and summer school for those who could probably be successful if they received some additional preparation during the summer.

> *We offer summer school for the students whom teachers identify in ninth grade algebra who probably could have taken it in eighth grade. We provide summer school as a way they can catch up in order to take geometry in tenth grade, precalculus in eleventh, and calculus in twelfth. If we can get fifteen students, we offer the class.*

College information nights are offered in the parents' native languages so parents can gain an understanding of the process, and we include information about how to attend college with varying residency statuses. This proactive approach builds readiness for students and creates choices for students who might not otherwise have had a choice.

Recruitment efforts do not end on the first day of class. As a principal commented, "We encourage our teachers to try not to scare students into wanting to drop during the first two weeks of class." Another principal added, "Our goal is not only to get them into the classes but to keep them in." On some of the campuses, summer reading lists were provided for English literature classes; however, none of these schools used the reading lists as a way to remove students from class. If students had not read the reading lists, they were encouraged to do so when school began.

> *We do all we can to convince students that it's in their best interest to stay in the advanced classes. We tell them that being in the top 10 percent will get you into college but having participated in the advanced-level classes in high school is what gets you out of college.*

Provision of Professional Development

The principals also recognized the importance of vertical team meetings to the improvement process and supported the vertical team's efforts through actions such as paying substitutes so the vertical teams could meet all day for planning. Teachers who were not currently teaching AP courses participated on the vertical teams in the professional development activities. This alignment in student expectations ensured a smooth transition from each course to the next. Although all administrators required the vertical team members to attend summer College Board institutes, administrators assigned both AP and regular classes to individual teachers so that the strategies used in the AP program would also be used in the regular-level classes. Each of the administrators had eliminated low-level classes and honors courses. Students took either regular-level courses, pre-AP courses, or AP courses. Advocating for student success included ensuring the strategies and materials needed to achieve increased student learning were available for teachers.

Strengthening Teacher Buy-In

The principal served as an advocate in promoting quality professional development. Teacher buy-in to the AP program was strengthened through ongoing professional development opportunities. As an administrator commented, "It is important to train the staff. . . . New teachers coming into the program have to participate in professional development. We work to assist teachers." Principals also emphasized that they celebrate success, although they were quick to stress that they do not look at the percentage taking the AP tests versus the percentage passing as the indicator of the AP program's success.

As another principal stressed, "We celebrate our 5's, but we also celebrate our 2's, and 3's and 4's. We know students are better off for having taken the advanced classes."

> *We don't care about percentages. We are inclusive. We hope the students take the test, but if not, it's OK. The percentage is not important to us. We want the students to take the advanced classes and to take the tests. If the students pass, that's great; but if not, they are still better off from the experience of the harder class.*

Pellicer (1999) maintains that administrators must "care enough to lead." In his book titled *Caring Enough to Lead*, he says, "The book is not just for principals or other administrative personnel, present or future, but for all those who feel a deep personal responsibility, a sacred trust, to provide the most effective leadership they can in whatever role they may find themselves serving" (p. xii).

In considering the role of principals in bridging the ELL achievement gap by increasing student participation and success in advanced-level classes, a similar statement could be made. The role of administrators in bridging the achievement gap is important and is a role that could be assumed by teachers, counselors, curriculum directors, or all others who, as Pellicer (1999) stated, "feel a deep personal responsibility, a sacred trust, to provide the most effective leadership they can" (p. xii).

School leaders must be prepared to implement essential processes and practices needed to bridge the achievement gap. They must acquire knowledge and skills in areas such as collaborative planning efforts, fostering strong relationships with all stakeholders, data analysis, authentic leadership that models and communicates a sustained focus on equity and excellence, advocacy for social justice, best practices for curriculum areas, and leveraging resources for goal attainment.

QUESTIONS TO CONSIDER

1. The mindsets of school leaders influence their actions. Consider the reasons given by school leaders for their own schools' success in strengthening a college-going culture.

2. Why is this an important consideration as ELLs transition from ESL programs to the acquisition of academic English?

3. What do you feel is your role in carrying forward the great promise of education for ELLs?

4. In serving as an advocate for student success, which tangible actions have you observed that have resulted in greater success for ELLs?

5. Which strengths will you build on as you serve as an advocate for all students?

3

Strengthening Knowledge of Second Language Acquisition

The focus of this chapter is twofold: (1) building the principal's and faculty's knowledge base of second language acquisition and (2) illustrating what the implementation of that critical knowledge looks like in the classroom. This chapter provides a road map, showing the stops along this learning journey and the direction one must travel to arrive at success in meeting the needs of English language learners (ELLs) in a schoolwide effort.

Principals and teachers are realizing that traditional, segregated approaches to teaching English as a second language (ESL) simply aren't working. In traditional models, the ESL teacher held sole responsibility for helping students gain English language proficiency, while the content teacher held sole responsibility for teaching content. Contemporary, more effective ESL models call for integrated approaches to language development in which students learn both content and language concurrently.

This approach requires that content teachers become more familiar with language acquisition and ESL teachers become more familiar with content knowledge. Principals and instructional leaders are charged with facilitating this learning process and, in many instances, are learning side by side with teachers. Three key areas provide a framework for building and strengthening the knowledge of language acquisition: (1) recognizing the problems of deficit thinking and challenging assumptions, (2) building knowledge of the second language acquisition process, and (3) promoting successful instructional and curricular practices.

RECOGNIZING THE PROBLEMS OF DEFICIT THINKING AND CHALLENGING ASSUMPTIONS

Deficit thinking occurs when educators assume student disadvantage and relate it to the student's cultural or social experience. In other words, it is the false assumption that "the student who fails in school does so because of internal deficits or deficiencies" (Valencia, 1997, p. 2). This kind of thinking places the responsibility for academic achievement solely on the student and does not recognize the need for structural or professional improvement to meet student needs. In Chapters 1 and 2, we addressed the role the principal plays in creating a culture of achievement for ELLs and in building the faculty's commitment to positive reform. If the paradigm shift from viewing bilingualism as a liability to an asset does not occur, knowledge of second language acquisition and best practices for ELLs cannot be implemented effectively.

Knowledge of second language acquisition builds instructional capacity to respond to individual students continuously, creatively, and immediately. Knowing basic theories of second language acquisition equips instructors and leaders to respond on the go, just as we respond to every student, every day, in every moment. However, this knowledge will not have fertile soil in which to thrive if deficit thinking is crowding the belief systems of faculty.

> *You can't stick your head in the sand and blame it on somebody. You get your hands dirty and you just keep asking the right questions and you just don't give up. You don't give up on the kids; you don't give up on the parents. There's no blame. It's no one's fault. You have to be able to lay your head down every night and say, "I did the very best I could for every student who I know needed help today." That's what you have to do. It's not about having a meeting. I heard a quote the other day that's my new favorite quote: "He who leadeth and no one followeth is just taking a walk." I think a lot of administrators are just taking a walk, going through the motions. They don't really have the passion. Nobody is on board, so it's just a nice little stroll through the park that doesn't change anything.*

Going through the motions of positive change for ELLs without addressing the challenges of deficit thinking is like, as this middle school principal so aptly states, taking a walk—a walk that doesn't change anything.

The question remains then, How does one address deficit thinking? As this principal states, "You just keep asking the right questions and you just don't give up." There are two phases to challenging deficit thinking:

1. Openly dialogue with your teachers first to understand whether they hold deficit views and what those deficit views are. Then, continue the dialogue, asking hard questions to challenge the deficit views.

2. Provide opportunities for teachers to learn more about their students. Teachers cannot recognize and draw on inherent strengths and hopes of students whom they do not know.

Phase One: Openly Dialogue

Teachers and leaders must challenge deficit thinking by remaining steadfast in their commitment to equitable education. As we engage in positive dialogue and ask the right questions, we challenge assumptions about students in a nonthreatening way. In addition, working to build a culture of high achievement and working with families and communities move a campus culture away from deficit thinking and toward high expectations.

An elementary principal explained that she engaged in continuing dialogue to challenge the deficit assumptions made about ELLs on her campus. She met with small groups of teachers and began asking hard questions.

> I asked my teachers, "What do high expectations look like? Should we have the same expectations for all students?" I was really surprised at the dialogue that came out of that, especially with one of the strongest teams of teachers. They gave more excuses: "This child is from a low-income family." "This child is a second language learner."

Opening a safe dialogue with faculty allowed this principal to understand the faculty's views, expectations, and beliefs. While building understanding, the principal challenged assumptions that were being made—all the while building teachers' openness to being responsive to ELLs.

> And so I said, "Okay," playing the devil's advocate. "You have a second language learner whose parents don't speak any English. They listen to Spanish-speaking television and Spanish-speaking radio, and this is the only place they have a good English model. Should you not have the expectation that they be able to compete with their same-aged peers? And if we don't do that, when will they ever get it?" And so I think those challenging questions challenge the status a little bit. I think those kinds of questions, those kinds of dialogues, challenge some of our discord. They give us all a chance to look at it from another side, another perspective.

Through continued dialogue, this principal challenged the deficit views that focused on what the teachers perceived the students as not having: a white, middle-class, English-only experience. Through continued dialogue, the teachers began to focus on what the students did have: supportive families, aspirations of opportunity through education, strong community networks, previous language experience that would transfer to learning English, individual goals and dreams, and individual funds of valuable experience and knowledge.

Phase Two: Provide Opportunities

Deficit thinking can be challenged at more individual levels by providing opportunities for teachers to understand their students' experiences outside of school. In another attempt to challenge deficit assumptions about ELLs, one district interviewed ELLs who had graduated from the district. The panel interview was conducted during a professional development session and taped for future use. In the interview, students described their experiences as they began school as recent immigrants in the district, what helped them succeed, and what hurt them. Overwhelmingly, students spoke to the frustration they experienced when they felt that their teachers did not know how intelligent they were. Their experience prior to developing productive English skills was that some teachers equated a language difference with low intelligence or a low skill level.

One student, who immigrated to the United States in middle school with a low proficiency level in English, described her segregated experiences in ESL classes: "I was used to being with all the kids, but when I came here we [the ELLs] were all together, all the time. All we did was low-level math, low-level science, low-level everything. I felt like I was just passing by." This student is now in law school at a major U.S. university.

A similar story was shared by another student who immigrated as an adolescent with low proficiency in English. When asked what he wished teachers had known about him while he was learning English, he replied, "I wished they understood that I was smart. Teachers should be patient and challenge kids. Instead, I felt like I was held back." This student is now an engineering student well on his way to graduation.

Teachers were responsive to the video, and after developing a beginning understanding of the students' experiences and their abilities when they came to the United States, teachers were eager to begin or continue conversations with their current students to understand their emergent bilingualism as an asset rather than a liability. If teachers do not speak the language of the students, this should not be a barrier to understanding. Community members, social workers, and other school faculty members can unite in the effort to learn about students and their language community. As students gain English skills and emerge from the silent period, if a respecting culture of high expectations has been established, students are eager to produce language and express their specific hopes and aspirations.

Recognizing deficit assumptions and challenging those assumptions are critical precursors to strengthening a faculty's knowledge of second language acquisition. Once an understanding of students' abilities has been incorporated as an additive component to the diversity of the school, more specific knowledge related to second language acquisition will be firmly established on a strong foundation. In addition, faculty will be better equipped to respond to the knowledge gained about second language acquisition.

For ideas about structuring difficult dialogues, see Chapter 6, "Resources for School Improvement in Meeting the Needs of English Language Learners." There you will find Tools 3.1 and 3.2, "Engaging in Difficult Dialogues," along with an explanation of the tools and an example of how one principal implemented the tools.

BUILDING KNOWLEDGE OF SECOND LANGUAGE ACQUISITION

Teachers who understand some basic tenets of second language acquisition and linguistics are prepared to respond to the needs of ELLs because they understand how to respond to students at varying proficiency levels in creative ways. Once teachers have a solid foundation of the processes of second language acquisition, then teachers are ready to create strategies that respond to the diverse linguistic needs of their students, and then administrators are able to recognize responsive strategies. It is unrealistic to expect that learners will be at identical language proficiency levels in any given classroom.

When teachers understand second language acquisition, they can align appropriate expectations to individual proficiency levels. Consider a content-area science classroom with students from varying first languages and at varying proficiency levels but with similar, uninterrupted backgrounds in schooling. These students all have background knowledge in scientific concepts, but they need a teacher who has knowledge of second language acquisition to (1) provide comprehensible input so they can continue to build their knowledge of science, (2) provide opportunities for all students to produce language at their level of capability, and (3) assess content knowledge using the English language tools the students currently have. Given these tasks, imagine a teacher using an identical strategy for each student. The results would not be effective. It has been established that using visuals is effective for ELLs. However, when and how one uses them largely are determined by each student's language proficiency level.

For a beginning student who has not yet fully developed receptive and productive skills in English, it is effective for a teacher to use visuals in instruction to provide comprehensible input and to use visuals in assessment to provide the student with the means to convey understanding. However, this would not be appropriate for a student with advanced fluency. For a student with advanced fluency, a teacher could use visuals to augment written text and increase comprehensible input. However, it would be inappropriate for a visual to be the sole unit of communication in an assessment because the student would not be increasing language skills. In other words, this technique would not be in the student's zone of proximal development (Vygotsky, 1978). Refer to Tool 3.4 for more information about the appropriateness of accommodations and modifications by language proficiency level.

A targeted strategies approach, aligned with specific language needs, yields more results than a shotgun strategies approach. Key concepts faculty must understand before beginning to meet students' needs include stages of second language acquisition, social language development versus academic language development, language acquisition versus language learning, and the role of the first language in second language development.

Stages of Second Language Acquisition

Steven Krashen and Tracey Terrell (1983) identified and explored the stages of second language acquisition. These stages (see Figure 3.1) are the foundation on which most states have developed their English language proficiency levels or descriptors in identifying students as limited English proficient and on which they monitor students' language development. Faculty members need a basic understanding of the stages of second language acquisition to respond to the linguistic needs of students. It is important to realize that while students progress in a natural order in their language acquisition, all students are individual learners and may or may not fall into the approximate time frames for English language development.

Figure 3.1   Language Proficiency Levels

Preproduction	
Characteristics	**Student Needs**
• Silent period • Beginning to understand English when they hear it but not yet ready to use it verbally • 0-6 Months • Up to 500 words in receptive vocabulary • May repeat key words or phrases but not verbally producing language	• Extensive graphic support • Highly contextualized, concrete learning opportunities • Safe, friendly, supportive environment • Opportunities for heavily scaffolded participation in class activities—at their readiness levels • Targeted first-language support for content-related objectives • Formative assessments modified to offer students either/or choices with graphic supports so students can show comprehension of content

Early Production	
Characteristics	**Student Needs**
• Beginning to come out of their perceived shells • Not only understanding English (reading and listening) but producing English (writing and speaking) • Minimal comprehension • Up to 1,000 words in receptive and productive vocabulary • Beginning to speak and write in short, one- to two-word phrases, often in response to direct questions	• Continued support as described in preproduction stage • Prepared sentence stems, enabling students to accurately show their content knowledge while also building academic language • Participation in choral reading of content-related texts • Very structured opportunities for language production within content • Extensive use of graphic organizers • Access to modified supplementary texts

Speech Emergence	
Characteristics	**Student Needs**
• About 3,000 words in receptive and productive vocabulary • Beginning to initiate speech and produce questions • Comprehension begins to increase exponentially • Beginning to write brief stories and paragraphs	• Continued support as described above with decreasing scaffolds • Continued graphic and video support for comprehension and assessment • Participation in paired or small-group reading • Opportunities to journal in English (provide extensive, less-structured production activities)

Intermediate Fluency	
Characteristics	**Student Needs**
• About 6,000 words in receptive and productive vocabulary • Beginning to produce more complex sentence structures • Initiating questions • Better able to transfer metacognitive skills to comprehend content because they are no longer in survival mode • Still often cognitively processing in native language	• Language production still contains many errors—continued encouragement to produce language, very targeted corrections so students continue to produce language • Increased emphasis on higher-order thinking skills • Increased emphasis on developing metacognitive comprehension strategies • Continued scaffolds to support comprehension and assessment • Additional processing time for comprehension and assessment)

(Continued)

Figure 3.1   Language Proficiency Levels (Continued)

Advanced Fluency	
Characteristics	**Student Needs**
• Near-native ability in English • Still developing academic language proficiency • Can take 5–7 years or more to fully develop advanced academic fluency	• Students may have been exited from limited English proficiency services—continued support in developing academic language proficiency • Continued graphic support, engagement, and semantic mapping to continue language development

ACTION POINT

Students should have multiple opportunities to speak, read, listen, and write in English, with support, in all content areas.

Students should be afforded opportunities to participate in each of these literacy areas at their readiness levels and in line with their proficiency levels.

This kind of differentiation is made possible through heterogeneous grouping, small-group activities, cooperative learning, formative assessments, and performance assessments.

All students learning English will go through the acquisition stages but at varying rates. Students also develop each literacy skill (listening, speaking, reading, and writing) at varying rates. For example, a student's stage of language acquisition for reading could be more advanced than his or her stage for listening. It is for this reason that many states, such as Texas, have developed distinct proficiency level descriptors for each literacy skill. Teachers then meet each ELL's linguistic needs at each proficiency level (reading, writing, speaking, and listening) rather than at a general level.

Teachers must have an understanding of each student's proficiency level in each literacy skill to design instruction and assessments that are scaffolded appropriately. The ESL or bilingual teacher assesses each student's language proficiency level using state- or district-approved assessments at increments determined by state and district policy. Classroom teachers receive this information from the ESL teacher and should use it. However, teachers are also afforded a forum to provide valuable information about language proficiency growth as they assess students formatively in the classroom. Providing students multiple opportunities to produce and receive language in daily classroom activities provides the teachers valuable insight into student language proficiency growth. Then, teachers can use students' language proficiency level ratings in each literacy skill as well as provide informal assessments designed to assess content in discrete literacy modes.

If the process is not carried out, students may not receive comprehensible input of content or may not be able to accurately show their understanding of content in assessments. The student's proficiency levels and the teacher's responsiveness to them are the keys to effective acquisition of both content and language.

It is important for faculty members to understand that linguistic difference is another dimension of student diversity. However, it is not the only dimension. ELLs retain individual learning differences, just as all students do. ELLs have individual learning needs, such as multiple intelligences and learning styles, in addition to linguistic needs. Therefore, all ELLs in the preproduction stage are not the same although their language development needs might be similar. Figure 3.1 is available for quick reference in Chapter 6 as Tool 3.3.

Social Language Development Versus Academic Language Development

All faculty members should be aware of the basic differences between social language development and academic language development. ELLs acquire social language much more quickly than academic language. Social language includes survival English or playground English—in other words, everyday English students use with friends, hear on television, or use in other informal settings. Krashen (1982) estimates that social language development takes one to two years, with language experiences dictating how quickly it actually develops. Academic language is the language of the classroom and of content. This language can take five to seven years to acquire. If appropriate linguistic scaffolds are not in place, academic language development can take much longer, but if the scaffolds are in place, it can occur more quickly.

Social language can develop rapidly when students are exposed to authentic, concrete social situations in which they must mediate the situation in English. As a result, students can appear to have developed a more advanced proficiency in English when assessed on their social language development. However, their academic language may not have developed to the same degree. Teachers should not be quick to assess a student's language proficiency in English based on the surface-level social language. Instead, teachers should understand that academic language development occurs at a deeper level that is not as apparent as social language, which students often produce more readily.

As a result, teachers must pay explicit attention to planning opportunities for ELLs to receive and produce academic language. Teachers might be tempted to make content language more comprehensible by making it easier or using what they perceive to be simpler terms. This should be avoided. While offering synonyms and more student-friendly terms is a crucial part of providing comprehensible input, failure to pay explicit attention to the academic vocabulary, syntax, and language use often found in content classes does not provide ELLs with equitable access to the curriculum. Unless teachers provide students access to higher-order, academic language, ELLs will have no way of developing the academic language skills necessary for future educational opportunities. Scaffolds should, of course, be in place to develop academic language. However, attempting to make language easier is not an appropriate scaffold because it does not provide ELLs with language skills necessary to learn content.

Language Acquisition Versus Language Learning

Krashen (1982) delineated the difference between language acquisition and language learning. In short, language acquisition is compared to picking up the language, much as one learns his or her first language, through an almost subconscious process of exposure and contextual use. In contrast, language learning is the explicit teaching of grammar and rules of the language. For our purposes in contemporary schooling, it is critical to understand that either extreme in the acquisition/learning continuum is not optimal for second language development. On the one hand, ELLs will not pick up or subconsciously acquire English language by being submersed in a content class ripe with language experiences. On the other hand, ELLs will not learn language by being placed in a segregated ESL classroom that focuses solely on English language drills and rules. The optimal learning environment for ELLs will provide a language-rich classroom in which students will be able to receive and produce English in a content area while also receiving explicit instruction in English. The key is to provide a meaningful context in which this language learning can take place. In addition, students should be provided opportunities to receive and produce academic language in a meaningful context. This two-way practice is essential for developing not only language but also deep meaning of content. See Tool 3.3 for a short sample of literacy engagement ideas for ELLs.

ACTION POINT

In a classroom in which students are provided opportunities to receive and produce academic language,

- principals should SEE students reading multiple kinds of texts aligned with the curriculum: textbooks, trade books, magazines, newspapers, Internet articles, and so forth;
- principals should HEAR students talking about content in multiple formats: to their peers in think-pair-shares, to their class in prepared statements or speeches, to their teacher in informal responses, to themselves as they work out a structured response using a sentence stem, together in a choral read, in a group in reader's theater, and so forth;
- principals should SEE students writing in multiple formats: in informal journals, as they prepare answers they will read to the class, in editorials about current events, in formative answers on personal dry erase boards, in formal essays, and so forth; and
- principals should HEAR materials for active viewing or listening: short video clips of content being studied, audio of literature, and so forth.

The Role of the First Language in Second Language Development

A student's first language plays a critical role in his or her English language development. Knowledge of, and language development in, a student's first language transfer to the development of the second language. It is for this reason that the ESL teacher should assess both first language and English proficiency. Although this is not always possible, it can be critical for a teacher to know which literacy skills have been firmly established in the first language. Scaffolds for transferring knowledge of the first language to the second language differ from scaffolds necessary to build initial literacy skills in the student's second language.

When we work with teachers, we often hear differing opinions of the role the first language plays in content instruction. When is it appropriate to translate? When is it appropriate to challenge the student to develop English language? This is where knowledge of each student's proficiency level and linguistic needs is imperative. For some students, a quick translation of a single keyword will give the student access to the rest of the content. For other students, it is appropriate to develop metacognitive decoding skills to gain the meaning of a word or phrase. If students are in a situation in which translation is readily available and they are provided translation at will, students can become conditioned to expect the translation. This does not aid development of English. Native language should be used strategically, as appropriate for the student's proficiency level and as appropriate for the learning and language objectives of the lesson.

> *I tell my teachers, if you're working on a lesson and the student doesn't understand strawberries and it is keeping the student from understanding the lesson, say fresas and move on. Otherwise, you have lost the student. Don't send the student to the dictionary unless you are working on dictionary skills. You can lose too much content focusing on something that requires a simple, quick translation.*

Aligning instruction to a specific language objective is imperative, as explained below. If the language objective for the content instruction in a specific lesson were to use context clues to gain comprehension of the word or phrase, then a translation would not be appropriate because the linguistic goal for the day would be to develop the student's ability to discern words in the English language. However, if this was not the language objective and the word or phrase the student was struggling with was preventing the student from acquiring the content, it would be acceptable to translate.

Of course, in some cases, teachers will not have the language skills for translation. In these cases, the student's first language may not be used to the extent that a more common language might be. It is important, however, to understand some key

ACTION POINT

Even in classrooms with multiple first languages, it is possible to note key features of first languages—syntax patterns, alphabetic principles, common positive and negative phonetic transfers, cognates and false cognates, keywords, and so forth. In a classroom we visited in Houston, Texas, with multiple first languages, the students highlighted transferable roots, suffixes, and prefixes in green and nontransferable ones in red. This was done in all student work and displayed consistently in student work in the classroom.

features of the student's first language to appropriately scaffold instruction and assessment. This knowledge can be gained while simultaneously building relationships with bilingual parents, students, and community members by simply asking. In a rural east Texas district, each week a native-language family night is held in Spanish. At family night, important district and campus information is shared. The focus of the evenings, however, is to develop parents' English skills. During the process, teachers and school leaders who are volunteering gain knowledge of Spanish. This knowledge is then shared in small learning groups. Similar responsivity and mutual learning are accomplished in the classroom as teachers note features of the first language and use this information to anticipate student difficulty in transference to English. In addition, small-group study with a teacher leader familiar with the first language is highly effective.

For example, Spanish syntax often requires that the adjective follow the noun rather than precede it. In English, we would describe the house as "the white house," whereas in Spanish, it would be *la casa blanca* or "the house white." This is an oversimplification of a complicated syntactical difference evident in all languages—not just in the placement of adjectives. Not only does this difference require extra processing time for students as they formulate their thoughts into English words, phrases, and sentences; it also requires that teachers know just enough about linguistic differences to recognize a developmentally appropriate linguistic "error." In times past, lack of knowledge of second language acquisition processes was cause for overrepresentation of ELLs in special education programs.

Teachers should also develop a basic understanding of cognates and false cognates in students' native languages. Cognates are words that are similar or identical in the student's native language and in English and have the same meaning. For example, *accident* in English and *accidente* in Spanish are cognates. False cognates are words that are similar or identical in two languages but do not have the same meaning. For example, *pregnant* in English and *pregunto* ("question") in Spanish are false cognates. Knowing cognates will help the teacher address potential difficulties and take advantage of knowledge transfer from the first to the second language. More often than not, students have knowledge of language structures, which can transfer to language structures in English. For example, prefixes, suffixes, and root words are common language structures that transfer in academic vocabulary because they are Latin based. For example, in English, the root *bio* means "life," just as it does in Spanish.

At all times, students' native languages should be honored and respected. Students should be encouraged to continue to use their first languages at home and with friends. It is critical for students—especially younger students—to realize that acquisition of a second language does not mean loss of the first language. Language is a critical component of culture, which in turn is a critical component of identity. Students who lose their languages or are made to feel that they are inferior can suffer detrimental effects to their identity development and sense of self (Suarez-Orozco & Suarez-Orozco, 2001).

At one school with an extremely diverse first-language population, teachers take the time to learn key phrases in the students' first languages. It has become the policy of the school to praise and affirm all students in their native languages. This action builds mutual linguistic respect in the classroom and builds a culture of an additive attitude toward bilingualism in which bilingualism is viewed as an asset. In addition, students are encouraged to share native-language translations of vocabulary in content area classes. Not only does this practice build a classroom culture of mutual respect; it also aids student knowledge transfer by activating background knowledge and forming meaningful connections with English vocabulary.

PROMOTING SUCCESSFUL INSTRUCTIONAL AND CURRICULAR PRACTICES

Having knowledge of second language acquisition processes and the basics of successful instructional practice prepares faculty to align expectations to student linguistic needs. Rather than using a purely strategies-based approach, which attempts to find the magic silver bullet to "fix" language issues, faculty should engage in a ground-up planning and instructional approach. In this approach, the faculty members promote successful instructional practices that are aligned with student needs. By designing the strategies to meet real needs, teachers can avoid feeling lost in the sea of ELL strategy resources.

We can have a million ELL strategy training sessions and I can buy ELL strategy books for all my teachers, but if they don't know why they should use them, when to use them, or how to use them . . . they aren't going to use them. We took a step back from this approach and started conversations about planning instruction, the information each teacher needs about each student, and how to modify and accommodate in an effective and efficient way. From there, my teachers had the knowledge they needed to pick strategies that made sense to them and to the students.

Align Instruction to the Student's Language Proficiency

Each teacher should develop knowledge of each student's language proficiency level and what the language proficiency levels mean. The principal should work to ensure that all ELLs' language proficiency levels are assessed and monitored in compliance with federal and state guidelines. Tool 3.3 provides a general overview of proficiency levels; however, different states have adopted different methods of English language proficiency assessment, which also correlate with various proficiency level descriptors (see Figure 3.2). Although different proficiency level descriptors exist, they generally are similar.

Instructional strategies should then be aligned according to individual learners' linguistic needs. For example, beginning students need heavier graphic support than advanced students. Advanced students can handle more complex text than beginning students. Beginning students will need scaffolding at their linguistic levels. The principal might observe teachers using sentence stems with beginning students who are structuring oral responses ("The answer is _____ because _____."). In the same class, the teacher might not provide sentence stems for more proficient students to structure an oral response but might provide those students with more complex linguistic cues when framing complex sentence structures in a written response ("After testing the hypothesis, we concluded _____. Our evidence showed _____.")

Understanding language proficiency levels is critical because what might help one student instructionally—such as extensive graphic support and simplified language for a beginning English speaker—can hold back another student, such as a student gaining advanced fluency. Teachers must respond to each ELL's diverse linguistic needs.

Align Assessment to Students' Language Proficiency

Assessment should also be aligned to proficiency level. As students are developing language, they often have receptive skills (listening and reading) that are more developed than their productive skills (speaking and writing). In other words, students understand more in English than they can speak or write in English. Therefore, students can gain content knowledge but may not have the English development to show that content knowledge. In addition, they may be processing the newly acquired content knowledge in their native language. However, they have not yet developed the English "channel" by which to show the teacher their new knowledge. This can be a very frustrating position for the student. Structured responses, pictorial choices, concrete manipulatives, and total physical response are among the assessment strategies teachers can use to scaffold student assessment of content. Again, assessments should be aligned to students' proficiency levels. It is appropriate to provide a beginning student pictorial, either-or choices; however, this expectation is too low for a student with intermediate or advanced fluency.

Figure 3.2 States' English Language Proficiency Levels

State	Name of State-Mandated English Language Proficiency Assessment	Proficiency Levels
Alabama; Delaware; Washington D.C.; Georgia; Illinois; Kentucky; Maine; North Dakota; New Hampshire; New Jersey; Oklahoma; Pennsylvania; Rhode Island; Vermont; Wisconsin; Wyoming	Assessing Comprehension and Communication in English State-to-State for English Language Learners (ACCESS for ELLs)	1–5
Alaska; North Carolina	IDEA Proficiency Test (IPT)	Novice Low (NL), Novice High (NH), Intermediate Low (IL), Intermediate High (IH), Advanced (Ad), Superior (Sup)
Arizona	Arizona English Language Learner Assessment (AZELLA)	Pre-Emergent, Emergent, Basic, Intermediate, Fluent
Arkansas; Iowa; Louisiana; Nebraska; South Carolina; Tennessee	English Language Development Assessment (ELDA)	Pre-Functional, Beginner, Intermediate, Advanced, Proficient
California	California English Language Development Test (CELDT)	Beginning, Early Intermediate, Intermediate, Early Advanced, Advanced
Colorado	Colorado English Language Assessment (CELA)	1–5
Connecticut; Hawaii; Maryland; Nevada	Language Assessment Scales Links (LAS Links)	1–5
Florida	Comprehensive English Language Learning Assessment (CELLA)	Beginning, Low Intermediate, High Intermediate, Proficient
Idaho	Idaho English Language Assessment (IELA)	Beginning, Advanced Beginning, Intermediate, Early Fluent, Fluent
Idaho	LAS Links	1–5
Kansas	Kansas English Language Proficiency Assessment (KELPA)	Beginner (Low, High), Intermediate (Low, High), Advanced (Low, High), Fluent

(Continued)

Figure 3.2   States' English Language Proficiency Levels (Continued)

State	Name of State-Mandated English Language Proficiency Assessment	Proficiency Levels
Massachusetts	Massachusetts English Proficiency Assessment (MEPA-R/W), Massachusetts English Language Assessment (MELA-O)	1–5
Michigan	English Language Proficiency Assessment (ELPA)	Pre-Production, Beginning, Early Intermediate, Intermediate, Early Advanced, Advanced (Proficient)
Minnesota	Test of Emerging Academic English (TEAE), Minnesota Student Oral Language Observation Matrix (MN SOLOM), K–2 Reading and Writing Checklist	1–4 (Reading), 1–5 (Oral Language and Writing)
Mississippi	Stanford English Language Proficiency Test (Stanford ELP)	Pre-Emergent, Emergent, Basic, Intermediate, Fluent
Missouri	Maculaitis Assessment of Competencies II Test of English Language Proficiency (MAC II)	Basic Beginner, Beginner, Low Intermediate, High Intermediate, Advanced
Montana	MontCAS English Language Proficiency Assessment (MontCAS ELP)	Novice, Nearing Proficient, Proficient, Advanced
New Mexico	New Mexico English Language Proficiency Assessment (NMELPA)	Beginning, Early Intermediate, Intermediate, Early Advanced, Advanced
New York	New York State English as a Second Language Achievement Test (NYSESLAT)	Beginning, Intermediate, Advanced, Proficient
Ohio	Ohio Test of English Language Acquisition Test (OTELA)	Pre-Functional, Beginning, Intermediate, Advanced, Proficient/Trial Mainstream
Oregon	English Language Proficiency Assessment (ELPA)	Pre-Production, Beginning, Early Intermediate, Intermediate, Intermediate, Early Advanced, Advanced (Proficient)
South Dakota	Dakota English Language Proficiency Test (DELP)	Pre-Emergent, Emergent, Basic, Intermediate, Proficient

State	Name of State-Mandated English Language Proficiency Assessment	Proficiency Levels
Texas	Texas English Language Proficiency Assessment System (TELPAS)	Beginning, Intermediate, Advanced, Advanced High
Utah	Utah Academic Language Proficiency Assessment (UALPA)	Pre-Emergent, Emergent, Low Intermediate, High Intermediate, Advanced
Virginia	ACCESS for ELLs, IPT, Stanford ELP, or district-selected English language proficiency test	1–5; NL, NH, IL, IH, Ad, Sup
Washington	Washington Language Proficiency Test II (WLP-II)	Beginning/Advanced Beginning, Intermediate, Advanced, Transitional
West Virginia	West Virginia Test of English Language Learning (WESTELL)	1–5

How will teachers know what is appropriate? The more advanced a student is, the more—and more complex—language he or she should be producing and receiving, with decreasing scaffolding. For example, an intermediate or advanced fluency student has the language skills to produce more—and more complex—language than a beginning student. Therefore, the teacher should align this expectation with the assessment. Similarly, a beginning student does not yet have the linguistic capability in English to produce or comprehend complex or lengthy structures. An assessment that requires this skill is not valid. Differentiation based on language proficiency is critical to both accurately assess and challenge ELLs.

Do Not Lower Expectations

ELLs have cognitive skills and functions—barring identified individual special needs—just as their native English-speaking peers do. While they may need scaffolds for comprehension and production in English,

ACTION POINT

Structured Responses: Provide ELLs sentence stems in which they fill in key vocabulary or fill in the blanks but do not have to create the syntax of the phrases or sentences.

Pictorial Choices: Offer ELLs graphic representations of the answer choices to remove confusion or misinterpretation from textual representation. This is similar to a word bank but instead is a picture bank.

Concrete Manipulatives: Students have the actual objects or representations and are able to create or manipulate objects to solve a problem. In math, ELLs might use equivalency cubes. In science, ELLs might order slides to show the proper phases of cell division.

The goal is to align the assessment with the level of language the student has. As the student progresses in language proficiency, more language is added to the assessment.

they are fully capable of cognitively processing content information. Lowering content curricular expectations for ELLs does not provide them equitable education opportunity. Too often, ELLs who are assessed in English on standardized tests are not able to fully represent the content knowledge they have and are prohibited from access to enrichment and advanced programs. For example, a student knows the material but may not understand the words on the test. As students acquire English, formal standardized assessments become a more valid portrayal of their content knowledge. However, as students are developing English, curriculum may be scaffolded for ELL access, but it should not be watered down, and expectations should not be lowered.

For instance, if English-proficient students are studying osmosis in science, ELLs will be studying osmosis as well and with the same content objective. Teachers without the skills to differentiate may be tempted to offer a worksheet to an ELL to color or copy. This is a watered-down expectation. A higher expectation is to offer equal access to the curriculum. If students are learning the process of osmosis, the teacher might find an animated explanation of osmosis for preteaching to ELLs. HippoCampus (www.hippocampus.org) is a free homework and study help site that we often use to access quick simulation videos. Some videos are available in Spanish. Regardless of the scaffold the teacher provides, the content expectation cannot be lowered. Doing so puts ELLs behind curricularly and sets them up for future academic failure.

Be Proactive About Challenges for ELLs in Content Area Classes

Waiting until ELLs experience difficulty with academic content puts ELLs in the situation of remedial education. However, being proactive about potential content challenges and accelerating learning for ELLs with a focus on their emerging bilingualism builds a solid foundation for future academic success. ELLs will likely have more difficulty with abstract concepts such as literary elements or ideas such as freedom or civil liberty. Instead of providing remedial or additional tutorials after these lessons, plan ahead to engage ELLs with concrete supports prior to and during the lesson. ELLs can be engaged with abstract concepts through techniques such as storytelling, personal examples, and short video clips to activate background knowledge. Planning proactively for ELL access to content area material will prevent a remedial approach to learning for ELLs.

We've really been working on background knowledge—activating background knowledge is so important. If the student has prior knowledge of a subject and you don't tap into that, all the knowledge and skills the student brings with him or her to your class is lost. Then, nothing transfers! Also, if the teacher doesn't make that connection, the student will. And if the student is going through the files in his or her brain and picks the wrong file, the student is in trouble, and the teacher is going to have to help the student attach that new knowledge to the right place. So we have made a campuswide effort to help each other develop our skills and find new ways to connect knowledge for our students.

Concrete Support for Abstract Concepts

As ELLs are acquiring academic concepts in content, it is imperative that teachers provide concrete supports. Realia (real objects), photographs, manipulatives, labs, video clips, and other supports can be used to create or activate background knowledge for ELLs. In one chemistry classroom with a large number of ELLs, the teacher explained the concept of diffusion by spraying perfume from her position in the front of the room. As students smelled the perfume in the room, they were to raise their hands and keep them up. The students were able to take the academic concept of diffusion and apply a concrete, experiential definition. In the previous osmosis example, the science teacher provided a concrete example with a video clip prior to providing more abstract discussions and examples of osmosis in the lesson.

Similarly, graphic organizers can provide tangible support for abstract, complex concepts. For example, a concept definition map (see Figure 3.3) helps construct ELLs' understanding of subtle connotations of words—an abstract level of understanding. Concrete support is important because then ELLs know the target area for the lesson and can connect it to knowledge they already have. Also, concrete support provides comprehensible input in instruction and can also be used to assess ELL student knowledge formatively.

Authentic Differentiation for ELLs

Authentic differentiation for ELLs means authentic knowledge of each student's linguistic needs. Obtaining this knowledge has traditionally been the role of the ESL teacher, who might have held sole responsibility

Figure 3.3   Concept Definition Map

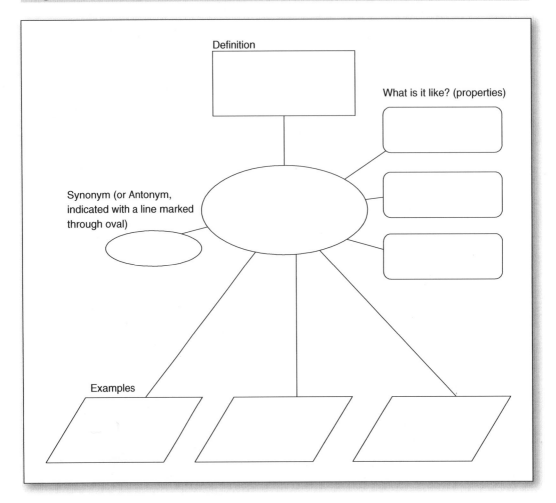

for gauging a student's linguistic needs. However, in more effective models of English language development in which ELLs develop language alongside content, content teachers need a grasp on each student's linguistic ability so they can differentiate authentically. The most effective mode for content teachers to achieve authentic differentiation is to provide ongoing formative assessments. Students are given multiple opportunities to produce language at intervals during the content area lesson, thereby providing the teacher multiple opportunities to gauge both student learning and language development. Not all ELLs need the same types of support. Authentic differentiation requires that the teacher know which scaffolds are effective for each ELL and the appropriate way to wean students from scaffolds. While myriad ELL strategy books are available (many of which are high quality), if the student's language proficiency and scaffolding needs are not considered and aligned with the strategy choice, the strategy becomes ineffective.

One Hundred Percent Student Engagement

Sometimes teachers encounter the pitfall of mistaking a lack of ELL student response as the silent period. While the silent period is a valid phase in second language acquisition, it should be a relatively short phase and should not be used to account for continued lack of student participation. If the silent period continues beyond a few months, explanations should be explored, such as lack of a supportive environment or lack of language support to develop English. Students who are in a supportive environment with scaffolds for interaction will engage with both language and content. Providing structured opportunities for students to produce language in the content area will assist in student engagement. If two-way engagement in content and language is not present, ELLs will acquire neither content nor language. Structured interaction is a planned, organized, and teacher-directed method for students to work together (see Figure 3.4). This is imperative for ELLs who need methods for lowering anxiety when working with other students, interacting in English, using potentially unfamiliar cultural elements of interaction, and interacting with new content knowledge. Teacher-directed structures provide a safety net for student-to-student interaction, increase student interaction, and increase language production and reception opportunities.

EXPLICITLY TEACHING LANGUAGE

VOCABULARY, SOCIAL CONTEXTS, IDIOMS, COGNATES

As previously explained, a distinct difference exists between language learning and language acquisition. While teachers should be providing meaningful contexts in which ELLs can actively engage in language and context to develop language acquisition, it is also important to explicitly teach certain language concepts. Key content vocabulary must be pretaught and reinforced, just as is expected with native English speakers. However, ELLs need instruction in more subtle and social meanings of words. For example, it is not acceptable to say "Hey!" to the school principal, and it is generally more acceptable to say this to a friend. Social meanings of language and appropriate times to apply formal and informal uses of language can be taught through content as students speak with each other and role-play different content-related scenarios. Teachers have integrated these types of language lessons into content through lessons that include role-playing conversations from different perspectives or writing different types of essays or paragraphs for different purposes. One particularly effective strategy is CRAFTS (P. C. Bellamy, 2005) or RAFT (Buehl, 2001). In this strategy, students in any subject area use the following acronym to create a product about content (see Figure 3.5):

Figure 3.4 Ideas for Structured Interaction Activities

"Find Someone Who"	Give students a scavenger list of things to find, for example, "Find someone who can name five members of the Kingdom Monera," "Find someone who can name three features of prokaryotes," and so forth. Students get one name per item and verify the accuracy of the answer (Cubitt, Irvine, & Dow, 1999).

Why this is good for English language learners (ELLs): This strategy promotes oral language. The questions are already written for ELLs, so they are practicing speaking. They are getting content and academic vocabulary (depending on the phrasing of the questions) reinforced as they hear answers. Students are also verifying answers, so they are practicing listening skills.

"Talk to Your Partner" or TTYP	Also called "Think-Pair-Share," teachers give students a moment to think about or write down a reflective answer. Student A gets an allotted amount of time to share his or her response. Then student B has an allotted amount of time to share his or her response. The teacher then can direct student B to share student A's response (and vice versa), or the teacher can open the floor to the whole group to share responses.

Why this is good for ELLs: ELLs are provided time to construct a response before having to produce the answer. Then, they get to practice the answer with their partners. Their partners can help fill in content or words if needed. This extra level of support and practice reduces anxiety before the students produce language for the teacher or the whole class.

"Pairs Check"	Student A solves the problem. Student B coaches. Students switch roles. After two problems are finished, each pair checks answers with another team. If answers are wrong, they redo. If answers are correct, they continue (Kagan, 1992).

Why this is good for ELLs: The ELL is reading as he or she is the coach and reinforcing or guiding student B, which requires language production, all while using academic language. Student A is receiving language from the coach and integrating instructions into the problem. This cooperative strategy also provides an additional scaffold for any comprehension gaps during direct instruction and adds an additional layer of formative assessment for the student.

"Write Around or Simultaneous Round Robin"	Students are seated at a table with pieces of paper. The teacher poses an open-ended question. Students begin answering (in text or pictures). After the time limit, each student passes his or her paper to the left and continues the previous student's response. The cycle continues until complete (Kagan & Kagan, 1998).

Why this is good for ELLs: ELLs are provided multiple opportunities to produce written language in an informal setting. In addition, they are provided multiple opportunities to read language that other students—both native speakers and other ELLs—produce.

"Numbered Heads Together"	Students are assigned numbers in their group. The teacher gives a problem. The group members "put their heads together" to solve the problem and teach to all members of the group. When the time is up, the teacher calls a number. The student with that number gives the answer (Kagan, 1992).

Why this is good for ELLs: In addition to providing another layer of support in case comprehension was missed during any direct instruction, this activity gives ELLs another chance to produce and receive language at their readiness levels. If an ELL is a beginner, the student can take the role of listener and be coached as he or she prepares to give an answer in case he or she is called on. If the student is an advanced student, he or she can take the role of teacher and prepare others. This activity allows for differentiation for all language proficiency levels.

Figure 3.5   CRAFTS Strategy

C	Context	What is the context of my writing? (issues, current events, problems, debates, etc.)
R	Role	Who or what am I in my writing? (astronaut, concerned citizen, advocate, etc.)
A	Audience	Who is my writing for? (neighbor, principal, school board, etc.)
F	Format	What form will my writing take? (pamphlet, editorial, diary, memo, advertisement, etc.)
T	Topic	What is the purpose and subject of my writing?
S	Strong Verb	Which verb describes the purpose of my writing? (*investigate*, *inform*, *teach*, critique, etc.)

CRAFTS is an excellent strategy for ELLs to develop understanding of different acceptable uses of language in different contexts within the parameters of an academic subject. This strategy also allows for differentiation for individual students, performance assessment, and generative language use.

Idioms—phrases that do not translate literally, such as "it's raining cats and dogs"—provide special challenges to ELLs. In one elementary school with which we work, the principal realized that many of the students—native English speakers included—did not know the meanings of many idioms. The school began an "idiom of the week" campaign. The principal would give the definition of the idiom at the beginning of the week, and the teachers helped to informally reinforce the idioms throughout the week. The students had fun with the creative new use of language, and it helped many ELLs become acclimated to an often-confusing literary device. Teachers should avoid using idioms when delivering lessons to avoid confusion. However, students need to be taught idioms so that they can have access to English social language.

Multiple Productive and Receptive Literacy Experiences

Students who are developing proficiency in a second language need multiple opportunities within each lesson to both produce and receive the target language. What would this look like? Examples? Sometimes teachers of ELLs do not want to put children on the spot or read their silence as shyness, and they do not promote chances for students to produce English both in writing and in speech. Engaging students in many chances to speak, write, hear, and read English within each lesson

ACTION POINT

Simply put, ELLs need to be talking about, reading about, listening to, and writing about content in English.

cycle is imperative to developing language development and providing comprehensible input. In our work with teachers, this has been the most important feature of lesson planning, delivery, and assessment for ELLs.

> *We have a joke that when you give a test, it is like an autopsy. How would you like for the doctor to wait for the autopsy before he or she diagnoses what you need? Instead, we have moved to make sure that our students have many, many chances to speak and write throughout every lesson. We make sure to break up our lessons into small chunks and give students time to Think-Pair-Share. During thinking time, students write out their answers. This gives the teacher time to check and validate student responses for ELLs before they speak. This has been very successful.*

CASE STUDY

The fifth-grade language arts teachers at Burlington Elementary School were worried about recent benchmark results that revealed that their ELLs were scoring poorly on some objectives. The principal, Ms. Jones, called the ESL coach, Mr. Smith, and the language arts teachers to dialogue about the concern. Mr. Smith began the meeting by asking, "What are our concerns? What is working to address them? What needs to be changed to address them?"

A conversation began in which the teachers revealed that ELLs were scoring poorly on objectives addressing the main idea, inference, and other higher-order thinking skills. A fifth-grade teacher stated, "No matter what I do, they just aren't getting it. I am so frustrated."

Mr. Smith said, "Tell us about what you are currently doing, and we can talk about how to help the students 'get it.'"

"Well, we read a passage, and then we work on test strategies to answer the questions that follow. They will usually get the comprehension-based questions, so I know they understand the passage," the fifth-grade language arts teacher explained. "I'm confident that the students are given comprehensible input, but they clearly don't understand to the level we need them to."

Another teacher responded, "I agree. Plus, I have a real motivation problem with my ELLs. It's like I can't get them to even pick up a pencil sometimes."

The other language arts teachers agreed in the ensuing dialogue that these were the typical issues they were having. A common statement heard during the conversation was, "I'm using pictures like we were taught in the inservice, but they still aren't getting it. I show the pictures of the vocabulary words, but it doesn't seem to be helping."

Mr. Smith thought for a moment and responded, "I hear what you are saying. Let me see if I have this right. You stated the students appear unmotivated; they are performing well on comprehension or knowledge skills, but they are not performing well on higher-order thinking skills. In addition, you are using a strategy that is known to help ELLs, but you aren't seeing the results that you want." The teachers confirmed that this was their area of concern. Ms. Jones suggested that Mr. Smith observe the students in the language arts classes and then meet back with the teachers to target an area of professional development. All agreed.

The next day, Mr. Smith observed the ELL students in the language arts classes, paying particular attention to their motivation to learn and access to and participation in higher-order thinking skills. Since the language arts teachers plan and team together, their lessons were aligned. The ESL coach observed the following in all classes:

- students were working from test-preparation reading passages;
- the teacher read to the students, or the students read silently;
- the complete passage was read before the students processed information;
- students answered a multiple-choice question individually, the teacher called on a student to share an answer, the teacher confirmed or corrected the answer, and the teacher explained the correct answer to the class; and
- students proceeded to the next multiple-choice question.

Following the observations, the team met again to debrief. Mr. Smith started the meeting by recapping what he was asked to observe and noting what he observed.

"We talked about the need for increased student motivation and increased achievement on higher-order thinking for our ELLs. In my observations, I saw that the students were not motivated and, on average, did not answer the questions targeting higher-order thinking correctly." From there, Mr. Smith asked the teachers if they agreed with his observations, which they did. After talking, the teachers worked together to plan lessons to increase student motivation and achievement related to higher-order thinking skills.

After going over the various passages the students had been reading during the observations, the teachers realized the passages were decontextualized and had little relevance to the students. This could be a contributing factor to the lack of student motivation and lack of access to higher-order thinking skills. The teachers talked and decided that providing the background knowledge or building the background knowledge could potentially take more time than they had with the students. As a solution, the teachers decided to build on knowledge they knew the students had. The students had recently been studying states of matter and changes in physical properties of matter. They decided that combining the language arts objective with a science objective would provide some of the missing background knowledge that might be preventing the ELLs from engaging in higher-order thinking skills. In addition, this approach would reinforce the skills from science and contextualize the skills from language arts.

The teachers decided to plan a lesson using the myth of Daedalus and Icarus. They could use the example of Daedalus's wax wings to reinforce changes in physical properties of matter; students should be able to predict the outcome of Icarus's flying too close to the sun. They could also use the example of the wet wings to show a change in physical property as the wings become heavy after Icarus falls into the sea. Students should be able to infer the reason Icarus cannot swim to safety after falling into the sea. In the future, teachers could work together to align the background knowledge in other subjects.

During the discussion, the teachers also decided that reading to the students was ineffective. The teachers had been doing that to keep the students on a similar pace. The teachers also decided that waiting until the entire passage was completed to assess student understanding was ineffective. To address both of these concerns, the teachers decided to try "chunking" the reading. After a short block of text, students could engage in informal assessments that would engage all literacy skills. Teachers would design creative, short, informal assessments for after each chunk. This would allow the teachers to differentiate for language proficiency level.

In addition, chunking the reading would allow the teachers to vary the way students read. For each section of text, the teachers would choose to have students read silently, partner read, choral read, or listen as the teacher reads. Combining the formative assessments with the chunks of text would give the students multiple literacy experiences while also giving the teacher valuable information about student understanding prior to the completion of the reading.

The teachers liked the ideas but were not completely sold on the implementation. As one teacher said, "This sounds great and all, but this sounds like too much. We've got testing coming up, and I want to make sure the students will score well! I don't know if we have time for this." Mr. Smith offered to work out the details and try the lesson with a class. Ms. Jones arranged for the other teachers' classes to be covered so they could attend the model lesson.

At the beginning of the lesson, Mr. Smith provided each child a small white board, a dry erase marker, and a stack of mini sticky notes. Mr. Smith showed the class a digital picture of a bird. Then he asked the students to make a list of the features of the bird's wing on the dry erase boards. As the class was writing, Mr. Smith walked around the room, reading students' answers and assisting in the process as needed. Next, Mr. Smith asked the students to compare lists with their elbow partners and add or change items on their lists. After this, Mr. Smith elicited whole-class participation to build a class list of the features of the wings. In the debriefing, the teachers noted that this task took only about two to three minutes and was an effective way to activate students' background knowledge.

From there, Mr. Smith guided the students through the reading, varying the way students read and stopping after each chunk of text—which ranged from one to four paragraphs. These stopping points provided Mr. Smith opportunities to formally assess student understanding. Students used their dry erase boards to write predictions, answer teacher-directed questions, note questions about words or confusion about events, and perform many other creative, engaging assessments. Students used their sticky notes to mark the sections or words in the text, write questions, and do other creative activities. Mr. Smith took care to align the questions with the objectives on which the students were not performing well—those that addressed higher-order thinking skills. In the debriefing, the teachers noted that this was more engaging than using multiple-choice questions, gave students opportunities to produce and receive English, afforded opportunities to differentiate at each student's language proficiency level while also affording whole-class instruction time, and was, in general, a more effective way to structure and plan the lesson.

Prior to one segment of the text, Mr. Smith—with permission from Ms. Jones—lit a birthday candle at the front of the class. Mr. Smith asked students to write words to describe the changes in physical properties they observed. In a follow-up activity, Mr. Smith asked students to talk with their partners about the causes and effects of the changes in physical properties. Mr. Jones designed this activity because he wanted to make sure students would have the tools necessary to infer the causes and effects of events in the story.

During the debriefing with the teachers, one teacher stated, "I can't believe it. They were doing everything that they weren't able to do yesterday. I thought that because many of the students came from impoverished backgrounds, they wouldn't have the skills necessary to make the inferences and answer the higher-order thinking skills. Plus, they were really excited to do it." From this point, Mr. Smith, Ms. Jones, and the teachers worked together to discuss the approaches Mr. Smith used that worked and why they worked. They also made plans to extend this professional development to the rest of the campus.

QUESTIONS TO CONSIDER

1. In the lesson, how does Mr. Smith meet the challenges the teachers expressed?

2. Which challenges does your faculty express in meeting the needs of ELLs? How can these challenges be addressed using the tenets presented in this chapter?

3. How do Mr. Smith and Ms. Jones work together to develop quality, embedded professional development that meets the specific needs of teachers and students?

4. How does Mr. Smith work to address the pressures the teachers were feeling from high-stakes testing without sacrificing quality instruction for ELLs? How can this be accomplished on your campus?

5. In which ways did you gain a deeper understanding of effective practices for planning instruction and assessment for ELLs?

6. How can your faculty work together to provide opportunities for ELLs to produce and receive English within content areas?

4

The Principal's Role in Building Capacity in the School Through Quality Professional Development

Schools are creative, generative, and responsive. Their leader's work is to cultivate learning at every turn, starting with their own.

—Donaldson (2008, p. 155)

In the previous chapter, we discussed the knowledge that principals and faculty need about English language learners (ELLs) and the language acquisition process as well as ways to gather information about the ELLs served by a campus or district. The next step—and the most challenging— is not only disseminating this knowledge to faculty members but also helping them develop and adjust their skills related to curriculum and instruction as they implement their new knowledge at the classroom level. During this instructional improvement process, faculty members need to be engaged as colearners as part of a continuous improvement cycle. In addition, it is critical that the school culture not evolve to place blame on students for the need to change. Instead, the school principal must work with faculty members to build their care, capacity, and confidence to respond effectively to the needs of ELLs.

Confianza is a Spanish word for which there is no direct English translation. Confianza is a combination of trust, mutual respect, comfort, familiarity, and understanding based on experience, which yields confidence—in you, in the other person, and in the relationship. Approaching professional development with confianza means not only that the principal has confidence in the faculty to implement the knowledge and skills necessary to authentically meet the needs of ELLs but that faculty members have confidence and trust in the principal to lead them, develop their skills, and provide them with the resources needed to provide equitable instruction to ELLs. Developing confianza in the culture of the learning community also means that the principal has developed the capacity of the faculty to work together to mutually develop and share skills. To have confianza means that the principal has developed a mutual professional relationship with the faculty that not only serves as the platform for quality professional development but also models the manner in which faculty will respond to students, parents, and the community.

CONSIDER THIS

- What characterizes best practices in responding to the need for all ELLs to grow in language and literacy development along with content acquisition?
- What characterizes the instructional changes that are needed for ELLs from a development perspective?
- How does approaching differentiated instruction for ELLs with an understanding of and development of confianza (a mutual professional relationship) strengthen positive expectations while also promoting the goals of equity and excellence?

BUILDING CAPACITY

The role of the principal in building capacity in the school through quality professional development is critical in creating positive instructional improvements to meet the needs of ELLs. The principal, as a leader of learning on campus, is charged with the task of leading instructional reform to foster quality teaching for a student population that current teachers may or may not have been adequately prepared to teach. Principals who recognize the problems of deficit thinking and challenge assumptions made about ELLs are in a position to provide specific professional development for teachers to transition from subtractive schooling for ELLs (Valenzuela, 1999) to education with equal opportunity and content rigor.

THE CHANGING LANDSCAPE OF PROFESSIONAL DEVELOPMENT

Before engaging in a professional development endeavor, principals should be aware that some teachers may have more traditional views of professional development in which "educators (usually teachers) sat relatively passively while an expert 'exposed' them to new ideas or 'trained' them on new practices" (Sparks, 1997, p. 2). Recent research on professional development has shown that the "sit and get" approach to professional development is ineffective (Arbuckle, 1997; G. T. Bellamy, Fulmer, Murphy, & Muth, 2007; Donaldson, 2008; Earley & Bubb, 2004; Glathorn & Fox, 1996; Hall & Hord, 2001; Kinnucan-Welsch & Jenlink, 2005; La Plant, 1997; Matthews & Crow, 2003; Murphy, 2005; National Staff Development Council, 2004; P. M. Short & Greer, 1997; Sparks, 1997; Tate, 2004). In addition, professional development involves developing the capacity of teams of individuals who are equipped and empowered to meet needs (Schlechty, 2001). Moreover, to improve school systems, building teacher and administrator capacity through professional learning is important at district, state, and school/community levels (Fullan, Hill, & Crevola, 2006). Effective professional development practices have made the transitions listed in Figure 4.1.

Figure 4.1 Changes in Professional Development Implementation

Movement From an Emphasis On	To an Emphasis On
• generic professional development	• subject-specific practices
• individual development	• organizational and individual improvement
• piecemeal, fragmented sessions	• a coherent design
• a district focus	• a school and a district focus
• adult needs	• student and adult needs
• transmission by experts	• studying practice by teams
• consultants as trainers	• consultants as facilitators
• professional development as an option	• professional development as a lifelong necessity

This chapter approaches the principal's role in building capacity in the school through quality professional development with the recommended professional development transitions mentioned in Figure 4.1 and describes the principal's role in strengthening the learning community through a "confianza approach," which builds professional collaboration and support.

Reflective Practice

At the core of an effective professional development program to improve instruction for ELLs is critical reflection. Reflective practice provides the opportunity to raise questions, analyze data, and problem solve and is a "potentially powerful avenue for school improvement" (Osterman & Kottkamp, 2004, p. 191).

A first step is reflective analysis of the specific areas of need for faculty professional development. In recognition that meaningful professional development must address the needs of faculty, including their issues and concerns (Sparks, 1997), the emphasis of professional development has changed from scheduling events to achieving results. In addition, educators must analyze students' performance data and consider obstacles to educational attainment that the schools themselves may be perpetuating (Nieto, 1999). For systemic changes to occur in school practices, policies, and processes to promote equity and excellence in secondary schools, leadership at all levels is needed (Scheurich & Skrla, 2003). Values of equity and social justice are important (Scheurich & Skrla, 2003), as is an inherent belief among school participants that change can occur (Dantley, 2005).

The change process is challenging and complex, and ongoing data analysis is critical in determining each step along the way (Fullan, 2007). In reflecting on data with faculty, principals should be careful not to stereotype students based on ethnicity or native language. ELLs do share similar characteristics, but they do not share identical individual identities or experiences. The authors of *Double the Work* emphasize that educators must view ELL students as individuals as well as a collective group (D. Short & Fitzsimmons, 2007). Although disaggregated data for the ethnic groups can be studied to identify needs and important next steps, ELL students represent many countries of origin and are highly diverse in income, citizenship, and mobility.

NEEDS OF ELLS TO ADDRESS THROUGH QUALITY PROFESSIONAL DEVELOPMENT

Figure 4.2 guides the first steps in assessing your faculty's professional development needs. It is important to first assess faculty needs and then prioritize these needs to develop a comprehensive plan of action.

Effective professional development designed to meet the needs of ELLs and affect ELL achievement and success at the classroom level should be designed with a dual focus or perspective. First, because many teachers—especially secondary content teachers—have had little to no preparation in language development, linguistics, or literacy in their subject areas, one focus of professional development must include imparting this content knowledge. However, teachers must be able to apply and implement this content in relevant and contextual activities at the

Figure 4.2   Assessing Professional Development Needs

Data to Consider	Questions to Ask	Potential Areas of Needed Professional Development
Classroom observations	Are English language learners (ELLs) engaged in learning in a similar manner as native speakers?	Differentiation for ELLs based on language proficiency.
Course enrollment equity audit	Are ELLs enrolled in advanced-level courses, regular courses, or remedial courses?	Having high expectations for ELLs. Understanding the difference between language proficiency and academic potential. Ways to encourage a college-going culture for ELLs.
Class schedules, classroom observations	Are ELLs isolated from peers whose first language is English? Are ELLs routinely homogeneously grouped within classes or otherwise separated or disengaged from the curriculum and instruction in content classes?	Engaging ELLs in equal curriculum expectations. Effectively integrating students with diverse language needs in the classroom and the curriculum. Facilitating meaningful classroom interactions between all students.
Discussions during faculty, department, or grade-level meetings	Does the faculty have preconceived, prejudicial, or stereotypical expectations for ELLs related to intelligence, ability, culture, and so forth?	Cultural proficiency and responsiveness training. Developing skills for cultural understanding.
Long-term achievement data for ELLs	Are ELLs who have been exited from English as a second language services performing at or above the level of their same-age peers?	Continued academic language support for ELLs with higher proficiency or for ELLs who are considered fluent.

classroom level. Therefore, a second focus of effective professional development for ELLs must include content-embedded application of these theories as well as an examination of the sociopolitical and cultural influences that affect teachers' beliefs about ELLs and could prevent effective implementation. The principal, as lead learner, must be able to keep both foci in constant perspective, communicate the clear vision of the relationship between language theory and content practice, and facilitate opportunities for faculty members to work together to develop and correlate their instructional skills with their new content knowledge related to language acquisition.

In addition to quality classroom instruction, or "just good teaching" (de Jong & Harper, 2008), ELLs need additional, explicit attention to their language development. Teachers must be able to match instructional and assessment strategies to fit appropriately with ELLs' level of English proficiency, and principals must be able to evaluate curriculum and instruction effectively for ELLs. Building these skills requires the development of faculty content knowledge related to language acquisition and linguistics. Teachers and administrators must become knowledgeable about language acquisition and "be prepared to address the diverse academic, cognitive, linguistic and sociocultural needs that ELLs present" (Kandel-Cisco & Padron, 2008, p. 237).

ASSESSING FACULTY CONTENT KNOWLEDGE

Most faculty members will need to understand the basics of language acquisition. This is an appropriate time to call in an outside consultant to build this content knowledge. If you have faculty members who possess this content knowledge, bring them in as resident consultants to build this knowledge. Most important, be sure the content is presented in a manner that enables faculty members to understand the implications at the classroom level, effects on student learning, and implications for effective assessment. Tool 4.1 provides an overview of general language acquisition concepts teachers need, specific topics, and implications for practice. This checklist will help you assess faculty learning needs and guide professional development.

MAINTAINING A COMMITMENT TO EQUITY AND EXCELLENCE

Meeting ELLs' needs requires providing cultural appreciation, relevance of content, and quality relationships, but it also requires paying attention to the attainment of academic content. As Nieto (1999) expressed, "The field has emphasized issues such as improving student's self-esteem, incorporating cultural content into the curriculum, and fostering interethnic friendships. Although these are indeed significant goals in multicultural education, the question, *But, can they do math?* has gnawed at me for years because it underscores the lack of access of bicultural students to high levels of learning and thus to expanded options for the future" (pp. 174–175).

In the twenty-first century, the question has become not only, Can they do math? but also, Do ELL students have adequate access to—and encouragement to access—algebra in the eighth grade as a gateway to calculus in high school (Conley, 2007)? Educational leaders play a key role in ensuring that all students attain content knowledge to high levels of comprehension and analysis (G. T. Bellamy et al., 2007). In meeting the needs of ELL students, many of whom are also low income, the goal is not only language acquisition but also high-level content acquisition (D. Short & Fitzsimmons, 2007). However, whole-campus intervention and knowledge of ways to meet the needs of ELLs are needed to support a culture of academic success for all students (Shefelbine, 2008). The goal of learning English must work in concert with the goal of acquiring academic content in schools (Nieto, 1999; D. Short & Fitzsimmons, 2007). To meet these goals, a school must ensure that ELLs do not remain isolated but are encouraged to access advanced-level courses, such as advanced placement courses. Furthermore, the school must build a whole-school culture that truly exemplifies a commitment to equity and excellence and is striving to truly meet the needs of all students (Shefelbine, 2008), and the school's principal is key in determining this culture (Leithwood, Seashore Louis, Anderson, & Wahlstrom, 2004). To shape the culture, quality professional development is needed (Sparks, 1997).

ESTABLISHING SUPPORT TEAMS FOR PROFESSIONAL DEVELOPMENT

To provide whole-campus intervention for ELLs to simultaneously acquire and develop language and experience academic success in a rigorous curriculum, support teams must be established for faculty to implement new knowledge and skills. The first level of professional development comes when faculty members learn language acquisition processes and teaching strategies; the second level comes when faculty members engage in meaningful actions to implement this knowledge. Teachers must collaborate with content or grade-level professional peers as well as with professional peers who are knowledgeable in second language acquisition processes. The principal can facilitate support teams through grade levels, teams, or departments. These support teams operate much like planning or curriculum teams but pay explicit attention to and provide support to each other for maintaining a commitment to equity and excellence as well as for planning and implementing language and content objectives effectively.

In Chapter 2, we discussed the importance of scheduling time for collaboration and planning as well as the importance of encouraging the English as a second language (ESL) teachers or other faculty members with language acquisition knowledge to take the role of teacher leaders. These two steps provide the structure critical to the faculty's implementing new knowledge at the classroom level. The ESL teachers and teachers who have gained knowledge and skills of language processes can lead support teams by grade level, team, or department. The teams can then work together to plan and implement best practices for ELLs as well as support each other as they build their capacity to integrate language development into their content areas.

In support teams, the ESL teacher or another faculty leader can help provide assistance in developing language objectives to augment content objectives. In addition, the support teams can work together to share strategies, discuss how to implement strategies, and evaluate strategy implementation. Teacher leaders of support teams can use Tool 4.2 (see Figure 4.3) to guide the process of implementation. Teachers can work together in this process, regardless of whether one or many teachers will implement the lesson that is being planned. All teachers will benefit from the model of planning and support. For example, teachers had previously attended a professional development session that taught that ELLs benefit from having real objects when learning concepts. Some math teachers had questions about how to actually incorporate objects into their lessons, especially when teaching abstract concepts. In a support and planning meeting, the teachers used a process and planning guide with these steps: assess, set goals, prepare, implement, and reflect.

Figure 4.3   Working Together to Plan and Implement Language Objectives

Steps	Purpose	Example From a Secondary Math Team
Assess	Discuss areas of instructional concern or English language learner instructional needs.	"Students do not have the language to understand the abstract concept we are teaching. One of the state standards we are about to teach is about representing relationships graphically and making predictions from functional relationships. I am having trouble explaining this."
Set Goals	Identify specific student needs and determine the required skill or strategy. Identify specific strategies or practices from professional development for teachers to implement.	Students need concrete examples to graph (student need). Teachers can provide objects students can manipulate (teacher strategy). Teachers can provide a concrete context so students can make predictions (teacher strategy).
Prepare	Collaboratively plan for the instructional activities and strategies. Create a model lesson plan together. Identify specific language objectives needed to augment the content objectives.	Teachers plan a lesson in which students use colored tiles to graph ratios of red tiles to the total number of tiles. This meets the state content standard and provides a context for prediction. The specific language need students require is to be able to express a prediction. Teachers plan to explicitly teach "If…then" statements to students so they can make predictions about the graph. "If the number of red tiles increases, then the graph will…"
Implement	Teach the lesson. If possible, have the support team observe the lesson. At a minimum, the English as a second language teacher or teacher leaders should observe the lesson.	

Steps	Purpose	Example From a Secondary Math Team
Reflect	After teaching the lesson, the support team reflects on these questions: What went well? + What can we do differently next time? Δ What was the effect on student learning and engagement?	The peer coach used the observation and reflection guide (Tool 4.4) to make notes and guide the discussion. Teachers decided that the sentence stem ("If. . . . then") worked very well, as did the concrete examples. Students achieved the learning objective and built their language structure to express a prediction. The next time, teachers decided to establish cognates during planning to help them express academic vocabulary and concepts. (For example, one teacher did not realize that "total" was the same word in Spanish and English. This helped students greatly. If she had identified this cognate ahead of time, she would have refrained from using synonyms such as "all of the tiles" when introducing the concept.)

After following this guide, teachers were able to see how to implement the lesson, what advantages (+) came from the lesson, and what they could change (Δ) for the next time.

PEER COACHING

Peer coaching is a nonevaluative way for teachers to observe and learn from each other. In addition to planning content and language objectives together, teachers have the opportunity to see how the plans are implemented. Teachers in this example used Tool 4.3 (see Figure 4.4), the Peer Coaching Observation and Reflection Guide, to take notes while observing the math lesson. The guide provides a nonevaluative way for teachers to make notes about the strategy the teacher tried. After trying peer coaching, one teacher stated, "Peer coaching has challenged me to be a better teacher. It has given me the freedom and tools to make changes in instruction that were desperately needed. Coaching has made me analyze my own lessons. I can't coach someone's lesson if I can't critique and evaluate my own lessons."

This reflective approach to implementation builds teachers' collaboration as they work together to improve instruction for ELLs. It also aids implementation because teachers have ownership in the process. In the first stage of professional development, teachers receive the knowledge they need to improve instruction. In the next stage, teachers receive support from each other in their content areas or grade levels to use the knowledge in effective and meaningful ways.

Following observations, teachers meet again to assess what went well with the strategy and what needs to be modified for the strategy to work in other lessons. Teachers are provided support from the ESL teacher or teacher leader. Approaching professional development implementation with professional peers leads to effective implementation while simultaneously building support for continued improvement.

Figure 4.4   Peer Coaching Observation and Reflection Guide

Planning and Standards

Which content objective does the instruction address?

Which language objectives are integrated into the content?

How do the content and language objectives complement each other?

+   Δ

Lesson Implementation

Strategy tried:

+   Δ

Strategy tried:

+   Δ

Student Engagement and Learning—How were English language learners given access to

- oral and written language practice?

+   Δ

- higher-order and critical thinking skills?

+   Δ

- active involvement in learning?

+   Δ

- effective, ongoing assessment of their content and language learning?

+   Δ

The following case study illustrates a change process that exemplifies the dual perspective of building faculty capacity to meet the linguistic needs of ELLs and emphasizing follow-through, implementation, and structures for support. This case study follows a peer coaching model of professional development. Classroom teachers and administrators attended two levels of professional development—a first level aimed at increasing content knowledge about language acquisition and a second level aimed at implementing the newly acquired knowledge into content areas. At the second level of professional development, a confianza approach was used as teachers and administrators gained confidence in their own and each other's abilities as they worked together to increase faculty capacity to provide effective instruction and assessment for ELLs. This case study illustrates the need to present content knowledge in contextualized, relevant, and subject-specific frameworks.

A CASE STUDY

SUSTAINED PROFESSIONAL DEVELOPMENT THROUGH COLLABORATIVE LEARNING

In a collaborative partnership project, six teachers from each of thirteen campuses attended professional development to obtain ESL certification and participated in on-site follow-up coaching and collaborative planning to meet the needs of the ELLs. The project communicated the message of additive rather than subtractive schooling (Valenzuela, 1999), seeking to eliminate deficit thinking concerning ELLs. The campus principal was a key leader in sharing this vital message. An academic culture that meets the needs of ELLs was strengthened by the collaborative partnership of a university and secondary schools.

The professional development occurred on two levels. First, ESL coaches attended joint inservice training at the university with higher education faculty and campus and district leadership. One participant noted that this level of training helped develop capacity to increase rigor at the secondary level because "having the conferences where the coaches and the principals hear—from a national perspective or from a regional perspective—what is happening successfully in other areas helps bring in the outside world." Second, ESL coaches worked together to implement follow-through at the campus level with their teachers in departments. At this level, coaches provided support to content-area teachers by assisting in application of the knowledge and strategies acquired at the university trainings.

Sustained Professional Development

To move practitioners beyond language acquisition in remedial secondary courses to participation in rigorous courses in preparation for college required a system of sustained professional development. Participants indicated that consistency in the professional development, the participants themselves, and the system of disseminating information in a trainer of trainers model developed a sense of security and validation. First, coaches became more secure because they knew that a cyclical system was in place to address areas of professional growth as they arose. Sustaining the development of teachers' capacity for understanding and implementing rigorous curriculum alongside language development gave a sense of community to the effort as a whole. As campuses consistently came together across districts, across content areas, and across grade levels, professionals developed networks of support. Participants began to understand the nature of professional development as a system. Instead of a traditional cause-and-effect approach to training in which teachers attend a training designed to treat a problem and then address the training in their practice, the systems approach emphasized the development and the process involved as professionals built capacity to integrate curricular rigor and language acquisition. Second, as professionals grew together, their practices as well as the process of development were validated. Using a systems approach to professional development (Senge, 2006) created a feedback loop for teacher leaders to share their growth with other teachers on their campuses. Participants indicated critical practices in the change effort, which enabled them to rise to the challenge of meeting high curricular standards for linguistically diverse students: embedded, ongoing professional development with specific, targeted goals as expected outcomes of training.

The systems approach to professional development and the manner in which educators went through training provided a framework for teachers to approach developing language while maintaining rigor and high expectations for secondary students. Participants indicated that the ongoing support for teachers exemplified the manner in which students should be provided ongoing support. In addition, the manner in which language acquisition was presented to teachers within their content areas so that it was relevant and contextual for them provided a model for teachers to present relevant and contextual learning activities in the classroom so their students could authentically develop and use academic language.

Embedded

Training for teachers to provide rigorous curriculum content alongside language acquisition was embedded into content areas. While conducting training in aligning content and language objectives, examples were provided in several content areas at general training sessions for ESL coaches. Coaches were able to access examples in multiple content areas. In addition, the network of coaches across content areas was able to dialogue to ensure that all coaches understood application in multiple contents. Coaches then met with secondary departments on their respective campuses to provide specific, in-depth training in aligning language and content objectives. Participants indicated that this approach was necessary to increase rigor in the classroom. Without this approach, many teachers indicated they would not be able to implement instructional and assessment strategies that increase rigor for ELLs. Above all, "support through application" was necessary for implementation at the classroom level.

Sharing training and giving support in application in specific content areas has prepared content-area teachers to teach content effectively to ELLs. Participants shared that prior to the embedded support, they were more likely to engage in segregated models of instruction for ELLs in which students were separated not only from the mainstream population but also from the mainstream curriculum. One participant noted, "We can't isolate these students anymore. . . . You have to send them out with support. You have to expose them to where they're going, or they're never going to get there. That was hard on some of our staff. It was [previously] a real comfort level to know you have eight students, and you're working on *See Spot Run*."

The nature of the change effort to set high expectations for ELLs is designed to provide the same support to ESL coaches and content teachers that they are expected to provide to students—embedded, relevant, authentic learning experiences to build capacity for high expectations in teaching and learning. As a result, the training has been implemented effectively at the classroom level.

Ongoing

In addition to being embedded, professional development was ongoing and cyclical. Campuses were provided an overview of strategies and techniques at the beginning of the year. Coaches attended three trainings at the university each year. Then, coaches worked with individual departments and individual teachers over the course of the school year. Participants indicated that the ongoing nature of the professional development increased their implementation at the classroom level. As one respondent noted, the ongoing nature of the professional development assisted in "filling in a lot of the gaps—you learn something and maybe you forget a percentage of it and then you learn something else and it adds to that portion that you forgot earlier." Just as teachers are expected to engage in learning cycles with their students, teachers engaged in learning cycles as they gained capacity to increase rigor and high expectations for ELLs in their secondary classrooms. This approach permitted the professional development to be aligned with constructivist approaches to learning as university faculty and inservice teachers worked together to discover effective ways to mutually develop language and content learning.

Again, this approach to teacher learning was then applied to student learning at the classroom level. Teachers in the change effort moved from a behaviorist approach to teaching ELLs. Previously, many teachers did not understand why afterschool or before-school tutorials or other modes of remediation failed to motivate students and failed to move their learning in directions that resulted in equitable access to rigor in the secondary curriculum. By embedding and sustaining teachers' professional development to build capacity to teach ELLs effectively, a more authentic, in-depth understanding of the development that must take place at the classroom level and the embeddedness of curricular expectations and language development began to emerge.

Structure for On-Site Coaching

One participant noted that the greatest influence on increasing effective secondary ELL instruction was related to the university's "giving each campus a coach to share and to encourage teachers with some practical strategies and hands-on activities." Providing support to teachers as they simultaneously developed language in ELLs and designed a rigorous curriculum required a structure for on-site coaching. This proved to be the greatest challenge at the secondary level, where it was more difficult for teachers to find time during the school day to work collaboratively. This difficulty required assistance from the principals to provide scheduling considerations for coaches to meet with teachers.

Scheduling

At the middle school level (grades 6 to 8), participants indicated that they were more readily available to meet during school hours to assist with teams of teachers or departments. The middle schools in the change effort had a team planning period scheduled into the day. When selecting coaches to work with teachers, consideration was given to the coaches' content areas so that coaches were available to meet with different teams during the day. This time with coaches was utilized to observe teachers who had implemented strategies or techniques that increased rigor alongside language development for secondary ELLs. Teams also met during the day to debrief with their coaches and reflect on lessons and the implementation of strategies and techniques.

At the high school level, ESL coaches observed teachers during their individual planning or conference periods, as common planning periods by teams or departments were not scheduled during the day. The change effort was implemented more quickly at the middle school level than at the high school level. This was due, in large part, to the challenge of scheduling collaborative time for teachers and coaches to collectively address the issues related to increasing rigor in the curriculum for secondary ELLs.

Repeatedly, secondary coaches and teachers at the high school level called for increased time for collaboration during which they could "plan and actually be able to practice those different strategies that we have learned in these wonderful workshops that we've attended."

Departmental

To address the issue of lack of planning time during the day, instructional leadership on the secondary campuses used time already scheduled after school for department meetings in content areas for coaches to work collaboratively with departments. A coach consultant from the university also worked with departments alongside campus coaches to address instructional concerns in each content area. On middle school campuses, one coach worked with the science and math content areas while another worked with the language arts and social studies content areas. High school campuses, with four coaches per campus, were organized along similar lines—generally with two coaches working together with science and math teachers and two coaches working together with language arts and social studies teachers. Coaches scheduled times throughout the year to work with departments after school to model lessons using language development within rigorous content standards. Teachers then implemented instructional techniques that the coaches observed during the school day. Participants indicated this approach was successful in gaining support from teachers in diverse content areas, such as science and math, who might have otherwise resisted the idea of integrating literacy skills and language development into their curricula.

Developing Relationship for Support

This approach to implementation of professional development cultivated a relationship of support between teachers, coaches, and the university. Teachers had ongoing, embedded support from their coaches, who had ongoing, embedded support from the university. Coaches indicated that one of the most valuable resources they gained, which they then shared with teachers, was the ability of the university to go "to the school to help us deliver lessons the way we should have been, especially with the teachers who really have never heard anything about English language learners before." Coaches stated that the relationship of support was successful in working with teachers because the teachers did not perceive the university assistance as an indictment against their previous instruction and assessment for secondary ELLs. Instead, university assistance was welcomed as the faculty worked along with the ESL coaches and their campus teachers.

The dispositions and beliefs related to educator expectations for ELLs must transition to implementation of high expectations and rigor for all.

> *I think that the ELL teaching strategies are very good teaching strategies. I let the teachers know that this isn't an add-on or something that's effective just for ELLs. Attending these professional development opportunities will really make your teaching better, and the strategies that you will learn will benefit all your students. I think we must provide teachers the opportunity to grow professionally and to be able to use as many strategies as they can. We talk about, "What are we going to do to enhance learning for the ELLs? Are we challenging the students?" We look at our achievement data and talk about ways we can more fully meet students' needs. I'm not going to prescribe something for the teachers. They're the ones with the special expertise.*

The processes involved in this shift must include embedded, campuswide, and content-specific support using both a cultural and an instructional coaching approach. The case study provided one example, but many other examples abound. Quality professional development is vital in developing the mindset and skills to foster both rigor and success for ELLs. Structures of collaboration, time within the school day, and ongoing coaching are also critical to strengthening teachers' skills in addressing the needs of ELLs. The principal's role is paramount in promoting a culture of high expectations that is characterized by academic rigor as well as academic support. In addition, the relationships of support and confidence built through a confianza approach of mutual respect are instrumental to transitioning smoothly to additive schooling for ELLs.

QUESTIONS TO CONSIDER

This chapter identified practices and processes that are making a difference in preparing educators to work more effectively with ELLs in one setting.

1. On your campus, which practices and processes are working most effectively in meeting the needs of ELLs?

2. What are areas to strengthen to ensure success for ELLs?

3. Which practices and processes are important to achieving the goals of a school-university partnership designed to improve teaching and learning in the university and school settings by preparing educators to work more effectively in meeting the needs of ELLs?

4. What are the critical roles you currently play in fostering successful professional development opportunities for faculty members?

5

Strengthening Home– School–Community– University Connections

According to the U.S. Department of Education (2001), approximately 10.5 percent of the students in America's public schools are English language learners (ELLs). A large portion of these students' parents do not speak English fluently, and "3.4 percent of adolescents live in linguistically isolated families" (Batalova, Fix, & Murray, 2007, p. 30). Although 65 percent of ELLs are native-born Americans, one or both parents may not speak English fluently (Editorial Projects in Education Research Center, 2009). To build culturally and linguistically responsive connections, it is important for the school principal to be cognizant of the demographics of both the campus and the community. From the Home Language Surveys that parents complete upon student enrollment, principals can identify parents' linguistic needs and use this information to hire bilingual personnel and translators. Outreach to ELLs' parents involves recognition of whether interpreters are necessary for communication with parents and whether classes are needed to teach English to parents.

A report to the Carnegie Corporation of New York titled *Measures of Change: The Demography and Literacy of Adolescent English Learners* indicates that limited English proficient students are more likely to live below the poverty line and less likely to have parents with high school degrees—two factors that correlate strongly with educational success (Batalova et al.,

2007). This situation greatly compounds the need for educational leaders to build rich partnerships with parents and communities. An enriching relationship between the home and the school improves communication, understanding, and achievement.

Chapter 5 focuses the principal's role in strengthening home-school-community-university connections. Practical suggestions are provided for enlisting parental involvement and parents as partners, developing systems for communication with parents and the community, and forming educational partnerships.

ENLISTING PARENTAL INVOLVEMENT AND PARENTS AS PARTNERS

Recently, educators in a small town near the university where we work asked us to talk to them about the culture of their ELL population. Historically, this geographic area had a very stable community and was only recently experiencing a demographic shift toward more second-generation Latino ELLs. The principal and assistant principal perceived an ELL parental lack of interest in educational matters. Through dialogue, we were able to discover that the leaders and the teachers had made the following assumptions about the parents of ELLs:

- Educators assumed that a lack of input into decisions about education indicated a lack of care or interest.
- Communication with Latino parents was most often in the form of letters sent home with students. If parents did not return letters or respond as desired, educators attributed this to a lack of care or interest.
- Educators assumed that the lack of parental attendance at events and lack of parent-initiated communication indicated a lack of care or interest.

In examining the first assumption, we asked the teachers how they knew the parents had a lack of interest. It was apparent that the leaders and the teachers were careful to demonstrate care for the parents and the students. They were passionate about their community—both the established and the newer members. However, their ideas about "how to do school" were so embedded that they were not able to interpret parental responses to school in new ways.

We gave the staff an analogy. Your daughter plays volleyball and is injured. Her doctor diagnoses suprascapular neuropathy. The doctor turns to you and your spouse and asks, "What do you think we should do?"

"Uh . . . whatever you think is best?"

In many cultures, teachers hold a professional status similar to that of doctors or lawyers. While they may not hold exactly the same social or economic status, they have the same perceived level of expertise. The cultural norm is that children are dropped off at school or leave the home for school to be placed in the hands of professionals who will not be questioned and who will educate the children appropriately. Lack of input into educational decisions in these cases does not signal a lack of care or interest; rather, it is a sign of respect and trust.

Does this mean that we should reinforce cultural divides between parents with different cultural expectations of schooling? Of course not. It means that, as leaders, we must first know all our parents and our communities well enough to understand their expectations of schooling. Then, we must enlist them as partners to ease the transitions into American expectations of schooling while maintaining respect for their expectations (it is nice to be respected and trusted as an educator, after all)—and increasing their comfort with becoming active partners. Would you be ready to give medical advice on the treatment of your child's suprascapular neuropathy? No, but if the doctor were to explain what the condition is, possible treatment options, and the risks and benefits of various treatments, you would likely start to form an opinion as a parent. Once the doctor validated your opinion, welcomed your input, and gave you a forum to share your view, you would be more willing to participate actively. This change, of course, would require communication.

The second assumption the teachers and the leaders made—albeit very innocently—was that sending a letter home with students to inform parents of an event or to request information or an action (such as help with homework or attention to reading time) was sufficient, especially if the letter was in both English and the native language. Sending letters was a firmly established and acceptable form of communication at this school. In fact, many of the parents had even attended the school themselves and knew to ask their children if the teacher had sent home a letter. However, after establishing more authentic communication with the newer parents in the community, the educational leaders discovered that these parents did not feel that the events were really for them. Also, the newer parents sometimes did not feel that they had the expertise to act on teacher requests such as helping their high school children with homework. This school's situation highlights the need for true personal contact, which has been repeatedly shown to be the most powerful form of communication with parents (Scribner, Young, & Pedroza, 1999).

Imagine if the doctor in the example above sent a letter home with your daughter after an appointment telling you and your spouse to start at-home physical therapy for the treatment of suprascapular neuropathy. Would you start the regimen? You might call the office and seek more information, but if you did not have the English language skills or if it were not an established norm in your culture to ask questions of a professional, would you make that phone call?

At the school in our example, the third main assumption of the educational leaders and teachers was that parents did not attend events and did not initiate communication due to a lack of care or interest. Although the leaders and teachers believed that the parents loved their children and wanted their children to do well, it was easy to explain parents' absence by filling in the blanks with excuses—without seeking input from the parents or the students. Such excuses ranged from "they are too busy" to "education isn't as important in their culture" to "they probably have to work" or "they have other obligations."

Before making assumptions, educational leaders and teachers should ask reflective questions to guide their next steps (see Figure 5.1).

Figure 5.1 Questioning Assumptions

Assumption	Reflective Questions
Lack of input into decisions	Are the parents made to feel welcome? Is child care provided? Are parents' ideas implemented, or are parents asked to serve as a "rubber stamp" on decisions?
Ignored letters	Has personal contact been made at least once? Are the letters mailed home or sent with students? Are the letters in the parents' home language as noted on the Home Language Survey for the child?
Lack of parental attendance	Are the parents made to feel welcome? Have work schedules been considered?

While parental absences could have been as simple as "they have other obligations," the implication of the oversimplified explanation is that other obligations were more important than attendance at a school event or initiating communication with teachers or school leaders. However, complicated cultural differences were often at play. After educational leaders initiated communication with parents, they discovered that parents didn't feel "invited" despite the letters sent home with their children. The letters sent home might have been addressed to the parents, but contact had not been initiated directly with the parents. The parents felt this was important. Does this mean that you must make teacher-to-parent contact each time you want a parent to attend an event? No, but it does mean that at this particular campus, in this particular community, the parents needed to feel invited at least once. Then, they would feel welcome and would be more likely to attend future events and to initiate contact with the school. It also means that educational leaders must recognize the diverse cultures of their school communities and that enlisting parental involvement requires a mutual understanding and comfort regarding such involvement and how it is initiated and maintained.

Educational leaders must also recognize that there are many forms of parental involvement. While we encourage parental involvement at school activities, the most powerful form of involvement is the ongoing conversations that a parent has with his or her child and the level of expectations that are communicated (Pena, 2000). Parents can be involved in their children's education even if they are not physically present at a school event. In a study of ten high school valedictorians who were migrant workers, all had the experience of someone who communicated high expectations to them on an ongoing, consistent basis (Treviño, 2000). As Marian Wright Edelman (1992), the director of the Children's Defense Fund, suggested, "children must have at least one person who believes in them. It could be a counselor, a teacher, a preacher, or a friend. It could be you. You never know when a little love, a little support will plant a small seed of hope."

> [From the parent of an ELL:] I fell through the cracks in the school system and struggled. I was pushed to the side, but I wanted my children to succeed academically. I planted the seed in their minds that an education is something that can't be taken away. Your diploma will always be yours. I felt like I was Johnny Appleseed planting the seeds of wisdom. My wife and I encouraged our children to keep going because there is a better future for them. Our four children have all graduated from college and have good jobs.

Although parental involvement influences children's academic success (Henderson & Mapp, 2002), parental involvement and involving parents as partners can take many forms. Olivos (2009) reports, "All too often experts provide educators with supposedly fail-proof suggestions and best-practice strategies for collaborating with CLD [culturally and linguistically diverse] families. As argued earlier, this approach is not in the best interest of educators or Latino families, for it tends to homogenize the latter group's culture, worldview, and life experiences" (p. 114).

Wide diversity exists in parents' backgrounds and experiences. There is no definitive list of ways to elicit parental involvement. In schools with fifty-two languages spoken, it is not feasible to translate messages into all of the languages. There are, however, places that are succeeding in reaching out to parents. An educator described the school's "Math Power Path Night." The displays of projects from the classes were arranged in a one-way entrance design so that parents could see the recommended course sequence for math and hear the students describe their projects as they followed the "Power Path." The principal thought perhaps 50 parents would attend this high school activity. Instead, over 200 parents came to the event.

A local educator placed an advertisement in the newspaper announcing a meeting to learn more about college enrollment. The meeting was being held at a community church and was conducted in Spanish. It was announced at church meetings as well as by personal outreach. The educators thought perhaps twenty parents would attend. Instead, over eighty parents were in attendance that night.

In the book *How It's Being Done,* Chenoweth (2009) reports on a school that holds Saturday workshops for parents to hear what children are learning in school, with curriculum nights every six weeks that hundreds of parents attend. The beginning sessions were much smaller, but as parents recognized the value of the sessions, attendance grew. In another school, parents go on field trips with students to colleges. Hamayan and Freeman (2006) offer multiple suggestions for reaching out to parents, including events involving the entire family, "make and take" events, technology classes, parent advisory committees, and bilingual storytelling nights. In multiple ways, schools are reaching out to parents and enlisting them as true partners in the children's education.

SYSTEMS FOR COMMUNICATION WITH PARENTS AND THE COMMUNITY

Multiple forms of communication can be established for outreach to parents and the community. The following examples illustrate what some educational leaders accomplished through a school-university-business-community partnership that implemented new formats and improved existing formats for student and parent outreach to prepare ELLs for enriching educational opportunities. These examples reflect important practices and processes to consider in parental outreach.

Personal Contact

A primary avenue of outreach to parents was personal, authentic contact with parents to share the importance of high academic expectations for students. One teacher commented, "Our parents, by and large, are very supportive. Once they know that you truly care, that makes a big difference. They're quite supportive." True caring, as displayed in positive actions to benefit students, was important in parental outreach.

To receive buy-in from your community and from your parents and your students, you first have to have buy-in from your staff. The staff has to believe in what you're trying to accomplish. Our administration was fortunate enough to have a group of people who truly believe in what we are trying to accomplish. One of the main things we have to do is walk, talk, and act in a way that people believe in what we're doing and that shows people that we believe in what we're doing. When we set those examples and we serve as a role model for the future of our children, then it's a lot easier for staff and parents to follow.

Keeping the lines of communication open was also important in sharing information with parents. In addition to the usual messages that were sent home with students, partner schools added communication tools such as monthly newsletters, notes in student agenda books that were signed daily, and a bilingual web page that was designed to keep parents informed. However, personal contact remained the most powerful communication tool.

> *One thing that we have found is personal contact is important. When sending notes and letters home, they don't always get there if it's just a standard letter addressed to everyone. We encourage our teachers to have personal contact with parents. Everybody got a call a few weeks ago when we were doing our benchmark testing. We asked our teachers to call parents and let them know that we're having this testing and to encourage the students to do well.*

Increased parental outreach through enhancement of traditional methods of parent communication has assisted in keeping parents informed of student progress, upcoming events, opportunities for involvement, and the continuing importance of high expectations and enrollment in rigorous courses.

Personal contact is possible—even when parents do not speak English. School leaders should work to make translators available. Teachers can work together in teams to make parental contact. During team meetings, individual student information can be discussed among teachers and then disseminated at one time to the parent. Providing one point of contact eases the parents' transition into the school culture—and eases the scheduling of the translator's time to work with the teachers.

Another avenue for personal contact with non–English speaking parents follows a model that builds capacity for parent and community leadership. Bilingual parents can be enlisted as liaisons for personal contact. Educational leaders can establish ongoing, parent-led meetings to address parent questions and concerns and share information through the bilingual parent liaisons.

> *I'm proud of the fact that we have increased enrollment in our advanced classes, especially with our ELL student populations. We've begun to really plant the seeds in some of these students' minds that they can go to college and there are no barriers. Also, we've been able to have parent nights where we've shared information about college. We have quite a few of our students who are first-generation college attendees. I think sometimes we, as educators, take for granted the need for sharing college information because we know a lot about going to college. But not all of our parents are well educated about what it takes to be successful in college and what they need to be pushing their children to participate in now to be successful in college.*

Implementation of New Formats for Parent Outreach

In our example, new forms of information sharing with parents included meetings away from school, specialized meetings, and a parent university. These forms of outreach strengthened parental involvement.

Meetings Away From School

While school meetings are the traditional strategy for discussing education issues with parents, additional avenues are available. Meetings with community service groups, civic organizations, the chamber of commerce, area businesses, and local churches provide access to many parents that may not have taken the opportunity to come to school. These settings are often seen as more comfortable for ELL parents. By taking the message to the parents, school personnel can demonstrate their commitment to high achievement levels for all students. Personal communication through announcements to church and civic groups can also provide a means for sharing information.

> I visit the churches, and usually on Sunday mornings, I get up and ask to be on the agenda, and I speak to the audience about the things that are going on in the school and how they can be involved. I tell them who they can contact if they need more information. I just spread the word everywhere I go basically, and that's very positive.

Sometimes parents would be willing to help if they knew of opportunities for involvement. In addition, once administrators have enlisted parental involvement, they have strengthened the parent network of support. Teachers and administrators were no longer taking the sole leadership roles in enlisting support; parents began to lead other parents because they had a network of trust and linguistic avenues that not all school personnel had.

> A lot of people have said, "Oh, I didn't know that. How can I help?" We've gotten a lot of support from our community that way, and then if they can't help—this has been the amazing part—if they can't help, those people know somebody who can help.

Specialized Meetings

Parents of ELLs may have unique needs in working with schools. For example, a local school held night meetings about college preparation that were conducted in Spanish for the Latino community. By doing so, school leaders acknowledged the families of Spanish-speaking parents as an integral part of the school community. School leaders overcame language barriers and communicated the school's message of high expectations. Many of the ELL parents were also relatively new immigrants to the United States and were unfamiliar with the educational opportunities available to their children.

The school principal should be aware of parent concerns and needs when scheduling specialized meetings for ELL parents. Not only should the meetings be presented in the home language, if only one other language besides English is represented, but the meetings should also focus on topics in which the parents are truly interested. These topics vary widely depending on the degree of diversity represented in the ELL parent population. In some schools, parents of ELLs have lived in the same neighborhood for decades and speak a language other than English at home. These parents likely do not need information about the culture of U.S. schools. In other schools, the parents of ELLs are refugees. Within each ELL population, there exists diversity as well.

Consider holding multiple specialized meetings in the community to talk with parents and conduct informal parental needs assessments for topics of interest. At the elementary level, topics have included curricular issues, literacy activities in the home, technology, and math night. At the middle and high school levels, topics tend to focus more on rigorous coursework and preparation for career and college readiness. For newcomer parents, the topics of language acquisition, U.S. credits and graduation requirements, and testing have always been critical.

As we continue to communicate a vision of rigorous coursework and college and career readiness in our work with schools, two topics invariably arise with parents: financial aid and residency status. These are two very sensitive issues—and are often informally cited reasons students give for leaving high school. They see these issues as barriers to postsecondary educational opportunities. Principals should couple a message of high expectations with a message of possibility; postsecondary education enrollment is both possible and fundable.

Sensitive residency issues. Sensitive issues of residency status often arise. While this issue should not arise in public school because all children are afforded free public education regardless of residency status, it comes up when the school is communicating a vision of high expectations and college and career readiness. The way we have addressed this issue is in generalities. We do not want to put any of our parents or students on the spot, we do not want to make assumptions about our parents or students, and we do not want to make them feel that they need to share any information with us that would jeopardize the mutual trust and respect that has made our partnership possible.

To address the issue, we gather information about postsecondary opportunities available in our state for students who are residents of the state but who have not yet attained citizenship. Texas, California, Utah,

New York, Washington, Illinois, Kansas, New Mexico, Nebraska, and Wisconsin currently offer in-state tuition for immigrant students who meet state requirements for residency status. We also bring representatives from local universities to explain financial aid and application processes for immigrant students.

Financial aid. Outreach to parents about how to complete financial aid forms can be scheduled and marketed aggressively through automated phone messages as a unique reminder of the importance of the sessions.

> Our alumni association has committed to every high school graduate that he or she will have a financial opportunity provided through our alumni association to attend college. Each student at our high school completes the financial aid form for student aid. We do that because the form is a treacherous course for moms and dads because so many of our parents have not attended college. We actually solicit our retired teachers' organization to come and put on financial aid workshops here after school at night for those moms and dads, and then we have a rigorous phone bank, and we call moms and dads at home and remind them of this financial aid workshop. We have about twenty computers that we use to walk the parents through the process to ensure that their sons or daughters are entered in the program.

> This past year, we have implemented an automatic voice call. Over the entire Christmas holidays, parents heard my recorded voice remind them of the financial aid workshops. That proved very helpful for our moms and dads. They just need those reminders. They want our students to go to college, but sometimes that fear about the ability to pay for college is overwhelming to moms and dads.

CONSIDER THIS

Consider actions of educational leaders that accomplish the vision of increased outreach to parents and community members.

- In your work in parent and community outreach, what has made a difference in your district or school?
- Brainstorm ways to reach out to parents.

The method of publicizing this workshop included use of the automated phone system that is generally used to report student absences.

The principal was very enthusiastic in reporting the school's emphasis on effectively preparing all students for postsecondary education. The principal described the philosophy that all students should be prepared for both access and success in postsecondary education and that the school can implement support systems to make this goal a reality.

Parent University

Another successful form of parent outreach was the parent university. Community and social service groups planned and hosted a day of information sessions for parents. Specific sessions addressed financial aid questions and postsecondary educational opportunities in the area. With this strong community support, parents received information about access to postsecondary education as well as financial resources available to support postsecondary education. Parents who had not attended a four-year college (the first-generation parents) developed a network of support to help them negotiate the process of preparing for and enrolling in postsecondary education.

FORMING EDUCATIONAL PARTNERSHIPS

Partnering with social workers and parent liaisons in schools is another way to share vital information with parents. In addition, schools can establish cooperative relationships between institutions and agencies that affect children's achievement. By staying aware of community events, school leaders can link to the events to strengthen a community-wide focus on education. They can also link to community-wide concerns. Working with businesses and universities enables schools to leverage resources for greater impact on ELL student achievement.

Since each partnership's focus may differ by context as individuals join together to meet local needs, each partnership may be different. Successful partnerships are characterized by a collaborative exchange of ideas, knowledge, and resources. The partnership is a reciprocal relationship based on shared goals. The Council for Corporate and School Partnerships (2002) stresses the importance of aligning the interventions with the educational goals of the school and district. Epstein et al. (2002) further suggest, "In a caring school community, participants work continually to improve the nature and effects of partnerships. Although the interactions of educators, parents, students, and community members will not always be smooth or successful, partnership programs establish a base of respect and trust on which to build" (p. 11).

Critical elements in a partnership's success include research-based leadership practices, flexibility, strong shared vision, lack of territorialism, positive sharing of results, and a sustained focus.

Leadership Practices

In current educational literature, successful educational leaders are characterized by such phrases as *servant leaders, leaders of leaders,* and *constructivist leaders* who display facilitation skills that are used in ongoing collaboration and dialogue with all stakeholders. Lambert et al. (1995)

refer to acts of leadership as "the performance of actions that enable participants in the community to evoke potential within a trusting environment, to reconstruct or break set with old assumptions, to focus on the construction of meaning, or to frame actions based on new behaviors and purposeful intention" (p. 47). Furthermore, according to Lambert et al., leadership knowledge, attributes, and skills include a "sense of purpose and ethics, facilitation skills, an understanding of constructivist learning, a deep understanding of change and transitions, an understanding of context, and a personal identity that allows for courage and risk, low ego needs, and a sense of possibilities" (p. 47).

Leadership for creating a culture of high expectations for ELLs involves multiple leaders engaging in the examination of school practices and processes that functioned as barriers to maximizing student growth. Distributed leadership contributes to strengthening a culture of high expectations. In distributed leadership, multiple individuals in various roles work intently to influence and achieve positive results (Elmore, 2000). Superintendents, counselors, teachers, community volunteers, and parents all assist in this effort with a focus on research-based practices.

> *What mattered was the fact that I had the security of knowing that you had looked at all of the data and research before we even got started. That was the one thing that was so important to me. Everything is research based. It's really research-based practices and initiatives.*

Flexibility

At the very beginning, when you are starting out, it is useful to know what others have learned in similar partnerships. As Silva, Weinburgh, Smith, Barreto, and Gabel (2008) report, "While the call for partnerships between public schools and universities is now several decades old, good exemplars continue to be needed" (p. 107). Flexibility in implementing school goals by using multiple strategies rather than one cookie-cutter approach is important. No initiative should be implemented without considering the needs and resources within the local context. Providing each partner school the flexibility to design the services in the way that best works for the school is important.

> *Along with leadership was flexibility. There was no rigidity. Because I did not know how to implement, I did not know what a valuable resource this was going to be. The leadership provided me with flexibility. The partnership leaders said these six school districts had to stay within these same guidelines, but there's flexibility as long as you can equate it to student success. That freed me from the tunnel vision that I had.*

A key element that contributes to the success of a partnership is local study of the data to determine what works within the context of a particular school.

> *What makes this whole project a success is that we have taken the same principles and been able to modify the implementation of the specific features of activities to what works within each local community with the available resources.*

> *As partners, we were always checking with each other because we were on a mission. It's like we were all going to Boston from our different locations going different ways, but we were always checking on each other along the way to see what methods we were all using. If something wasn't working, then we knew not to go there. So the strong partnership was very instrumental.*

A Strong Shared Vision

A clear vision for the goals is important to a successful educational partnership (Council for Corporate and School Partnerships, 2002). The partnership should remain focused on goals through the collaborative processes of the partnership.

> *I think a strong partnership has helped us to maintain our focus. A strong cohort creates strength. We always knew we had someone who was similar to us. Even though we were all so different, there was still that similarity. There was someone to call and say, "What about . . . ?" I cannot count the times that I've picked up the phone. There was always someone there to rely on. The leadership and collaboration with postsecondary partners have also been important.*

Lack of Territorialism

Turf wars can characterize an unsuccessful educational partnership. In a successful partnership, collaboration and a willingness to build on successes are important (National Association of Partners in Education, 2001). As a partnership coordinator shared, "Lack of territorialism by each partner was important. We all openly shared ideas."

> *I also think a lot of what we did helped to build a more well-rounded student, as far as not just the academic background but also being more involved in other extracurricular activities besides sports. This partnership has helped to broaden students' horizons.*

Ultimately, as Negroni (2002) stressed regarding partnerships, "funding may come and go, staff members may come and go, but when schools and communities work together to weave a network of support for young people, their personal and institutional relationships endure" (p. 285).

In an effective school-university-community-home partnership, leaders care about the partnership. This is evident, for example, by attendance at collaborative planning meetings, leadership institutes, and board of directors' meetings. Although some individuals will move from the district or campus leadership roles and new administrators and coordinators will join the planning team, attendance and participation at the collaborative meetings can remain strong if a core group remains. Structured opportunities to come together to share ideas can be maintained over time. The momentum of the partnership is increased by the positive results that are attained and shared through graphs, oral reports, and written reports. An advisory board member asked at the first board meeting, "When do we see the charts of the positive results?" The partnership leaders took his words as a challenge and reported annual benchmark results on multiple indicators of the improvement gains in student achievement.

> **CONSIDER THIS**
>
> - What do you view as the leader's most important roles in an educational partnership?
> - How do the experiences voiced by the participants in the partnership above compare with your experience?
> - How can partnerships assist in meeting the needs of ELLs?

CASE STUDY

INSTRUMENTAL PRACTICES IN SUSTAINING THE COMMITMENT TO PARTNERSHIP GOALS

In building the capacity to sustain positive results, sharing information from national and state reports to raise the bar in secondary schools is an important practice. Michael Fullan (1993), a leading writer on educational change, discussed the importance of linking to external efforts in the initiation of a change effort and suggested this practice as a way of building momentum. In partnerships, we have found that linking to national and state initiatives is important not only in the beginning phases of the change effort but also throughout the process of reform and in sustaining positive results. National and state reports continue to emerge that can be used in discussing the need for creating and/or strengthening cultures of high expectations in secondary schools. It was important to share these reports widely with school leaders and to discuss the implications for practice.

In an information age, it is important not just to learn once but to keep on learning. Yogi Berra (Berra & Kaplan, 2001) summarized this need by saying, "You always learn by doing, but you also learn by learning, if you know what I mean" (p. 33). It is important to provide ongoing opportunities for study and dialogue. In our partnership, we achieved dialogue through monthly meetings with partnership coordinators, monthly meetings of campus councils, biannual meetings with a board of directors, and biannual leadership institutes with all council members. Creating structures for collaboration provided a framework to assist in ensuring that processes of dialogue, reflection, planning, and evaluation occurred.

We focused on both national reports that support the need for enhanced academic preparation in secondary schools and state reports and initiatives that promote a culture of high expectations for all students. Being in a state with a high-stakes testing emphasis, we recognized the need to prepare students to do well on the state's accountability measures as one more incentive for our work.

Focus on Systemic Change

During our first partnership planning meeting, educators identified the importance of focusing on systemic change with the recognition that change would not occur immediately. The partnership focused on developing a system of high expectations for all through services to students, parent outreach, professional development, community and business involvement, and evaluative processes. Targeting all students with school-wide intervention efforts was critical to achieving the necessary buy-in of project participants. In addition to allowing districts to provide direct services to all students in the grade levels served under the project, the partnership affected the entire system indirectly through the professional development of educators across grade levels and roles and through intervention activities. As a superintendent commented, "High school has a college day where all wear something from the college of their choice to encourage students to think about postsecondary education. We have expanded this program into the middle school. We are trying to start the mindset for all students to attain a postsecondary education. It is the little things together that bring about systemic change in the direction that we are trying to go."

Enacting changes in policies and practices is also a part of achieving systemic change. For example, a superintendent stressed, "Locally, we changed the process of attaining grade points to a system based on pre-AP [advanced placement] and AP course completion with additional points for AP if they take the test. We are trying to prepare more students to enroll in these classes. What will be required for high school graduation is more strenuous than ever before. If we do not start in the prerequisite grades, students will not be prepared."

Vertical teaming became important to the process of achieving whole-school reform. As another superintendent emphasized, "The partnership provides the link to pull the pieces together, bringing together students, parents, the community, schools, community colleges, and universities. It provides a sense of direction."

A common focus is essential in achieving systemic change (Scheurich, Skrla, & Johnson, 2000). The partnership helped by providing resources and a common focus on high academic achievement for all students as they prepared for the demands of the twenty-first century. A superintendent commented, "The project has revitalized and energized me. We feel we are now headed in the right direction. Help is on the way, and the cavalry is here."

Kozol (2001), in his address at the National Conference of Education, suggested that metaphors for school leaders should be warriors, poets, and spiritual leaders instead of CEOs concerned only with profit margins and bottom lines. As educators who are committed to educational excellence for all students, the partnership provided a foundation for systemic change.

Ongoing Communication

When communicating the needs and the benefits of systemic change, sharing promising practices throughout the change effort was important in influencing a positive shift to a culture of high academic expectations. As the partnership was implemented, several promising practices emerged. The partnership linked with the community and businesses in joint planning efforts, including the establishment of scholarships for students who demonstrated financial need and were graduating under the Recommended or Distinguished Graduation Plans, a parent university that offered sessions of interest to parents, and job shadowing that provided opportunities to students. Parent, community, and business involvement was achieved also through parents' nights, college visits, newspaper and media coverage of activities, and a website for students, parents, and the community to access information pertinent to project goals. Services to students included tutoring, mentoring, college visits, job shadowing, transition minicamps, and counseling on college admission and financial aid.

In addition to promising practices that emerged from the partnership with business and community groups, promising practices in the effort to influence systemic change occurred. A continuing emphasis on making instructional changes by emphasizing subject-specific professional development resulted in increased numbers of teachers trained in pre-AP and AP strategies. In addition to pre-AP and AP training, a comprehensive professional development plan included vertical team training and meetings and paraprofessional training. In summary, creating a culture of high academic expectations involved ongoing communication of the benefits of the project, the needs being addressed, and the link to national and state initiatives.

A Focus on Positive Relationships With Students and Parents

Research indicates that financial aid information is not enough to increase students' college-going rates and success (Gladieux & Swail, 1998). More important as a catalyst for students' future plans for college is having relationships with caring individuals who supply ongoing support and encouragement in the process of helping students academically. The partnership adopted the philosophy that positive relationships contribute to student success in preparing for postsecondary education and in creating a culture of high expectations, and it therefore established a structure for mentoring programs with mentor training to ensure that relationships developed in an ongoing manner.

Community and parent outreach was needed to strengthen school-home relationships and to increase the knowledge level of all stakeholders regarding the availability of financial aid and the recommended courses for college preparation. Student success is fostered when the community and parents are involved in the educational process in a meaningful way (Reyes, Scribner, & Paredes Scribner, 1999). In addition, the community afforded many opportunities for students to see the relevancy of learning to future careers, which increased student motivation to succeed. Session presentations about partnership goals, financial aid, and course-taking information for postsecondary education were provided to mentors. Session presentations were made to parents and community members at area churches and to school paraprofessionals and community groups such as the Rotary Club, Concerned Black Men, and the Junior League to encourage participation in the mentoring program.

As another way of providing personal outreach to build positive relationships, the largest of the partner high schools established a mentoring/advisory program for all students in the school. Each faculty member, including each counselor and administrator, was assigned a group of fifteen students. The faculty member met with the students on a regular basis and monitored their academic experiences. These personal experiences in small advisory groups broke down the anonymity of a large high school and helped students to succeed. As a superintendent stated, "Education really goes back to relationships. That's the bottom line. It's not so much textbooks and curriculum as it is the relationships that teachers have with students to push us to be the best that we could be, to challenge us to move forward, and to have high expectations for our life and to reach those expectations."

The partnership recognized successes through celebration programs to acknowledge mentors for their work. Celebration of the processes an organization values is an important part of influencing cultural change (Deal & Peterson, 2009). Communication is an ongoing process. Finding ways to build and sustain relationships was vitally important to this partnership.

Working in Concert With Local Goals

Another important practice in building the capacity to sustain a cultural reform effort is to work in concert with other local efforts to improve academic performance in schools. One principal stated, "Our district was looking for ways to raise the bar." A superintendent added, "We had already set a goal to increase advanced placement and pre–advanced placement enrollment. When this partnership came along, it seemed a perfect way to implement this." Another superintendent added, "Our district had already started the vertical team process, but the partnership provided a way to sustain this effort." A principal further elaborated, "The partnership provided another tool in our arsenal to help students succeed to high levels." He added, "It's amazing what can be accomplished when no one cares who gets the credit."

The partnership leaders achieved positive results by working in concert with all of the other school-improvement initiatives in the districts; creating a culture of high academic expectations was not done in isolation. Powerful examples of the positive practices that occurred in participating schools are illustrated by a partnership teacher who stated, "First, as a group we established a vision that set high standards for our students. By raising the level of academic expectations, students are meeting the challenges. Our pre-AP and AP programs are inclusive rather than exclusive. We have set up vertical teams of teachers who have spent many hours planning and collaborating. We have been provided the opportunity for initial and ongoing professional development. We schedule frequent opportunities to communicate with parents and community members on the value of the classes."

Still another teacher offered as a word of advice to others, "Jump in! The water is fine. Expect more. Demand more from your students. You will be surprised. They will rise to the level of expectations." Another teacher added, "I am proud to be a part of an initiative that is successfully preparing today's students for college as well as for life." Linking to local efforts to improve the academic achievement level of students, a culture of high expectations was attained.

This partnership sought to prepare students for both access to and success in postsecondary education. Through the combined efforts of teachers, administrators, counselors, parents, community groups, businesses, a community college, and university partners, students received a "convergence of expectations" (National Commission on the High School Senior Year, 2001) for increased academic achievement. The efforts reflected a convergence of actions that served as a powerful force to positively affect students' opportunities in life. A university president shared his strong commitment to the partnership by stating, "Our work is about helping individuals to manifest their potential as human beings. What could be more important than that?"

The partnership sought to achieve systemic change to strengthen a culture of high expectations whereby increased numbers of students would take advanced-level courses in preparing for college, would recognize that college is possible and needed, and would complete the preparatory steps for postsecondary admission and success. Systemic change was evidenced by an interconnectedness of practices, resources, and policies in support of a common goal. Toward achieving the central goal of improving students' preparation for access to and success in postsecondary education, the partnership sought to work in concert with other school improvement efforts as an integral part of the school.

Education partnerships are ultimately relationships. Bauch (2001) emphasizes that educational partnerships are "built on social interaction, mutual trust, and relationships that promote agency within a community" (p. 205). From this study of an educational partnership, overall recommendations include the following: (1) provide a consistent focus through sustained leadership; (2) implement a structure for collaboration for planning interventions and analyzing evaluative data; (3) achieve synergy by working in concert with other key initiatives in the community, nation, and state that parallel the goals of the collaborative; (4) provide ongoing communication of the program's vision and the results being achieved; (5) rely on data-based decision making and targeting benchmark goals as vital factors in increasing commitment to the reform effort; (6) participate in shared professional development that is specifically focused on the attainment of project goals; and (7) distribute leadership from the university, school, and community for project success.

The needs of the twenty-first century and the changing requirements of the workforce demand increased academic preparation if students are to be prepared for future endeavors. The partnership sought to strengthen a schoolwide culture of high expectations for all students wherein participation in postsecondary education was not a plan for a few but the goal of all. Multiple interventions were planned locally by the partnership schools to affect the participation and success of students in advanced-level courses. In considering what mattered for this secondary school-community-university collaborative partnership in strengthening a college-going culture to prepare students for access and success in postsecondary education, multiple factors emerged. However, ultimately, the success of the partnership could be linked to one essential element. That is, the members of the partnership cared about the initiatives and were willing to put forth the sustained time and effort to ensure that the partnership achieved identifiable results.

QUESTIONS TO CONSIDER

1. Brainstorm ways that a school-university-community-business partnership could assist in meeting the needs of ELLs.

2. If you have worked in a school-university-community partnership to better meet the needs of ELLs, in which ways did your experiences mirror those described here?

6

Resources for School Improvement in Meeting the Needs of English Language Learners

You must trust and believe in people or life becomes impossible.

—Anton Chekhov

THE GREATEST RESOURCE

In schools, you must trust and believe in students, teachers, parents, and communities, or the hope that makes growth possible diminishes and school becomes a building of work instead of an ideal of possibility. The synergy that is possible when people come together is a too-often untapped resource.

The greatest resource in the community of learners is trust. Trust is inherent in communities that share similar backgrounds. We often do not recognize it as trust—we recognize it as familiarity; we trust the other person is familiar with our situation and will respond accordingly. When we encounter others with diverse experiences—languages, countries of origin, ethnicities—there exist an unfamiliarity and, by extension, a mistrust. This mistrust does not always manifest from a negative experience but from the fear of misunderstanding or lack of familiarity. This can be overcome—quite easily—by building a larger, inclusive school community based on understanding. Teachers and leaders who understand language acquisition processes and the cultures of their students can understand their students and can therefore respond to their students.

In Chapter 4, we shared that *confianza* is a combination of trust, mutual respect, comfort, familiarity, and understanding based on experience, which yields confidence—in you, in the other person, and in the relationship. When this kind of relationship is established in an inclusive learning community—principal, teachers, students, parents, and community—everyone takes care of one another. A system of checks and balances develop without the sense of monitoring. Instead, this system is a cohesive, mutual network of support and collaboration with an identical goal—student success and achievement.

However, to make this relationship a reality, leaders and teachers must build understanding. By working with students, parents, and community, understanding of culture and community expectations will be gained. Additional resources are needed to build faculty knowledge of specific knowledge and skills related to language acquisition. In addition, we recommend processes for bringing faculty to understand new cultures and ways to approach pedagogical practices. This chapter provides resources and tools to implement the ideas presented in the previous chapters.

BOOKS AND WEBSITES

Books

- *Teaching Reading to English Language Learners: A Framework for Improving Achievement in Content Areas*

  Margarita Calderón (2007) provides a lesson-planning framework, complete with strategies, for integrating language development into content areas. The approach is appropriate for all grade levels and content areas.

- *English Language Learners: The Essential Guide*

  David and Yvonne Freeman (2007) developed an accessible introduction to language acquisition and implementation of the theory into classroom practice.

- *Sheltered Content Instruction: Teaching English Language Learners With Diverse Abilities*

  Jana Echevarria and Anne Graves's (2007) new edition of *Sheltered Instruction Observation Protocol* is accessible to all content areas and grade levels. This book provides an introduction to language acquisition in addition to suggestions for implementation.

- *Differentiating Instruction and Assessment for English Language Learners: A Guide for K–12 Teachers*

  Shelley Fairbairn and Stephaney Jones-Vo's (2010) book offers a professional development approach for differentiation. The authors introduce understanding individual students' linguistic and cultural needs, language proficiency descriptors, and differentiation and scaffolding in a diverse classroom.

Research Reports

- *Schools Moving Up—West Ed Diverse Learners*

  http://www.schoolsmovingup.net/cs/smu/view/tpc/8

  This site provides multiple resources, including "tips to go," webinars, and articles related to teaching English language learners (ELLs). This is an excellent resource for principals to share during professional development.

- *Succeeding With English Language Learners: Lessons Learned From the Great City Schools*

  http://www.cgcs.org/publications/ELL_Report09.pdf

  The Council of the Great City Schools' report disseminates excellent information for leaders interested in what separates great schools for ELLs from the rest. The practitioner-friendly report provides principals and educational leaders with snapshots of four successful school districts with high populations of ELLs and provides actionable steps for replicating successful practices.

- *What Are We Doing to Middle School English Learners?*

  http://www.wested.org/online_pubs/PD-10–02-full.pdf

  This case study of middle schools in California offers recommendations and best practices for school leaders interested in implementing promising practices for ELLs.

Websites

- Center for Applied Linguistics

  http://www.cal.org/resources/pubs/phrasebooks.html

  There are many resources in the general resources page. Most helpful to us have been the phrasebooks, which list common phrases. They are available, at no cost to download, in ten languages. The phrasebooks are helpful for educators, students, and families alike.

- Colorín Colorado

  http://www.colorincolorado.org

  This bilingual website for families and educators of ELLs contains a wealth of information—from research and reports, to webcasts, to classroom ideas, to parental outreach.

- SEDL

  http://www.sedl.org/pubs/free_ell.html

  Free resources in the ELL section of SEDL's website include briefs and reports as well as professional development resources and summit proceedings.

- ESOL Tapestry

  http://tapestry.usf.edu/esol-resources.html

  This amazing list of content-specific resources provides principals and teachers a comprehensive resource for curriculum, instruction, and assessment.

- HippoCampus

  http://www.hippocampus.org

  HippoCampus provides animated, rigorous academic lessons in algebra (English and Spanish), American government, biology, calculus (English and Spanish), environmental science, physics, psychology, statistics, and U.S. history. This is an excellent site for teachers to use to retrieve online graphics and video for instructional support.

CHAPTER 1 TOOLS

Tool 1.1 Comparing Content and Language Objectives Verbs

Use this tool to help faculty become familiar with language objectives. Just as teachers are expected to activate learners' background knowledge, good professional development activates teachers' background knowledge. Build on teachers' understanding of Bloom's taxonomy (Bloom, Englehart, Furst, Hill, & Krathwohl, 1956) to transition teachers into the verbs of language objectives.

Tool 1.2 Crafting Language Objectives

After transitioning teachers into the verbs used in language objectives, use the chart in Tool 1.2 to work with your faculty to craft language objectives that align with the content objectives. After becoming more familiar with the language proficiency levels, differentiate the objectives for proficiency levels a teacher might have in the same class.

TOOL 1.1 COMPARING CONTENT AND LANGUAGE OBJECTIVES VERBS

Content Objective Verbs		Language Objective Verbs*
Content objectives are crafted and aligned with cognitive performance verbs (Bloom, Englehart, Furst, Hill, & Krathwohl, 1956)		Language objectives are crafted and aligned with linguistic performance verbs and phrases
Knowledge: define, describe, draw, find, label, list, locate, match		**Listening:** listen, recognize, point, show, follow direction, identify implicit ideas and information heard in . . . , demonstrate listening comprehension by, use (media source) to learn/review . . .
Application: choose, make, produce, solve, show		**Speaking:** pronounce, repeat, discuss, respond, state, restate, summarize, explain, tell, share, use vocabulary, agree, disagree, express opinions about
Analysis: classify, compare, differentiate, examine, infer, relate		**Reading:** read, identify, skim, explore
Synthesis: combine, compose, construct, design, organize		**Writing:** write, create, contrast, compare, classify, record, use simple and complex phrases to write about . . . , narrate, describe, explain
Evaluation: argue, assess, predict, rate, select		*Language objectives are aligned with each student's individual proficiency level as determined by the state's language proficiency assessment

SAMPLE CONTENT AND LANGUAGE OBJECTIVE

Content Objective**		Language Objective
Given a compass and a straightedge, the student will be able to construct a congruent triangle. **Content objectives remain the same for all students.		**Speech Emergence:** The student will be able to orally **restate** the construction of a triangle using the academic vocabulary: vertex, point, width, point, arc, original, congruent, compass, equal, side, and length. **Intermediate Fluency:** The student will be able to orally **explain** the construction of a triangle using the academic vocabulary: vertex, point, width, point, arc, original, congruent, compass, equal, side, and length. Refer to Tool 3.3 for a preview of the stages of language proficiency levels. Why are expectations different for students in intermediate fluency and speech emergence stages?

TOOL 1.2 CRAFTING LANGUAGE OBJECTIVES

Content Objective	✛	Language Objective
Using the current newspaper, identify three constitutional rights currently being protected or questioned by the Bill of Rights.	**Writing**	Use the sentence stem to craft a complex sentence for each of the three examples: This event is an example of _____ because it is about _____.
Using the six characteristics of a ballad, identify the elements in "The Ballad of Birmingham" (Randall, 1969).	**Listening**	
Identify the major causes of the American Civil War.	**Speaking**	
Compare the characteristics of the kingdom Monera and Protista.	**Reading**	
Apply distributive law to algebraic expressions.	**Writing**	

CHAPTER 2 TOOLS

Tool 2.1 Student Data Gathering

Home language surveys and state and federally required language testing provide one dimension of understanding a student. The principal, together with the English as a second language coordinator and classroom teachers, can use Tool 2.1 to create a multidimensional picture of each ELL.

Tool 2.2 Advocacy as an Everyday Process

Advocacy sometimes connotes picket lines and bullhorns, but this is not our definition. On the contrary, it is asking questions, promoting equitable education, and drawing people together. Principals can use Tool 2.2 as a reflective piece or a guide to embed advocacy as an everyday process.

Tool 2.3 Mini–Equity Audit

This mini–equity audit can provide a snapshot of the programs and resources to which ELLs have access. The mini–equity audit is a starting point for providing access to rigor and high expectations for all students.

The mini–equity audit should also consider former ELLs—students who no longer receive formal limited English proficiency services. These data will reveal if the campus and district are serving ELLs and providing true access to rigor and high expectations. These data can be difficult to track since federal regulations require tracking for only two years after the student exits limited English proficiency services.

The mini–equity audit is meant to be a reflective tool, but it can also be converted to a quantitative piece by using percentages of students on applicable questions.

TOOL 2.1 STUDENT DATA GATHERING

Student Name		Considerations/Goals
Country of Origin		
Native Language		
Parents' Language(s)		
Language(s) Primarily Spoken in the Home		
Native Language Proficiency		
Student Interests		
English Proficiency Level (Reading)		
English Proficiency Level (Listening)		
English Proficiency Level (Speaking)		
English Proficiency Level (Writing)		
Previous Experience in School		
Other Special Needs		

TOOL 2.2 ADVOCACY AS AN EVERYDAY PROCESS

Advocacy can mean studying the school's data to identify "hot spots" or areas of concern. Advocacy begins with posing questions:

What are the inconsistencies or concerns?	
Have we enlisted the help of translators from the community or hired aids if we do not have enough bilingual teachers?	
From the benchmark testing, have we disaggregated results?	
Have we hired tutors for students? Which personnel are still needed?	
Have we secured resources? Which resources are still needed?	
Are there achievement gaps by student groups?	
Are there interventions for all students needing help?	

What does it mean for advocacy to serve as an everyday process?	
Reflect on the actions needed in your school to better meet the needs of English language learners.	
What could be done, starting tomorrow?	
What would be long-term goals?	

Asking all of these questions and more is part of serving as an advocate for ELLs. The principal studies the student data from a commitment to assist all students to go as far as possible in academic performance. The authentic leader dwells in possibilities while serving as an advocate for the students in meeting their needs.

In an urban elementary school with a high ELL population, three tenets are the hallmark of the elementary school:

1. Learning should be fun.

2. Parent involvement is essential.

3. Learning is lifelong.

The principal was instrumental in engaging students in authentic learning activities rather than drill-and-kill worksheets. In addition, the principal fostered, supported, and reinforced their implementation:

- Rocking chairs were provided in the hallway where parents were invited to come and read with the children.
- The principal encouraged action research with teams of teachers sharing their results.
- Articles were provided at the front office for parents to take.
- An entire hallway was decorated to represent countries represented in the school.
- An international post office was established to send and receive letters with questions about the countries. A student could pose a question, and another student would mail the reply.

Advocacy takes many forms, but it is always based on caring (Noddings, 1984). For ELLs, advocacy for the students can mean securing resources as needed. It can mean brainstorming ways to better meet student needs. It can mean knowing the law and enforcing it. It can mean being a personal cheerleader for each child, providing encouragement and support and serving as a model of an ethic of care (Noddings, 1984).

If the leader is authentic and believes in the importance of the work being done, the advocacy won't happen just one time. The principal will be a sustained voice on behalf of children.

When working to create a culture of high achievement for ELLs, teachers, parents, community members, and students recognize clearly whether the principal's words are congruent with his or her actions. For example, if the principal says that we need to meet the needs of all learners, when the teacher requests resources to assist in meeting ELLs' needs, the principal secures them. When the principal voices a concern about increased parental involvement, he or she is present at the parent advisory meetings, the programs, and the community events. Serving as an advocate for the students and school is an everyday reality.

TOOL 2.3 MINI–EQUITY AUDIT

These student groups . . .	African American	Asian/ Pacific Islander	Hispanic	Native American	White	English Language Learner
are provided challenging and high-quality instruction.						
are provided access to comprehensible instruction.						
are equitably represented in resource allocation.						
are represented in parent advisory groups.						
are represented in the curricular materials.						
are achieving high standards on campus indicators of success (report cards, benchmarks).						

(Continued)

TOOL 2.3 MINI–EQUITY AUDIT (Continued)

These student groups . . .	African American	Asian/ Pacific Islander	Hispanic	Native American	White	English Language Learner
have established home-school-community networks.						
have access to school materials and resources in a language they and their family can understand.						
are represented on the faculty.						
are enrolled in advanced coursework (pre–advanced placement, advanced placement, honors, etc.).						
are taking the SAT, ACT, or other required admissions tests.						
are attending college/postsecondary or other school-to-work transitions.						

CHAPTER 3 TOOLS

Tools 3.1 and 3.2 Engaging in Difficult Dialogues Explained

In this tool, we provide a sample for initiating a structured, difficult dialogue with your faculty with the understanding that it would need to be adjusted to fit the climate of the group with which you are meeting and the culture of your faculty. We use five general guiding questions from which principals can open the floor to dialogue, or they can craft more specific questions to probe particular areas.

Tool 3.1 Engaging in Difficult Dialogues Example

In Tool 3.1, you are provided an example of a dialogue a principal implemented with her faculty, with notes about the methods she used for implementation.

Tool 3.2 Engaging in Difficult Dialogues Template

In Tool 3.2, you are provided a template for a general dialogue to implement with your faculty, with space for notes about methods for implementation and notes about the discussion you have with your faculty.

Tool 3.3 Language Proficiency Levels Quick Reference Guide

Tool 3.3 provides a quick reference of language proficiencies. This should be used in conjunction with Tool 3.4 to differentiate for ELLs.

Tool 3.4 Quick Reference Guide Modifications for English Language Learners (ELLs)

Tool 3.4 assists principals in knowing what to look for when assessing what are appropriate modifications for ELLs at different proficiency levels.

TOOLS 3.1 AND 3.2 ENGAGING IN DIFFICULT DIALOGUES

In Chapter 3, we discussed the need for the educational leader to engage faculty in difficult dialogues to move away from deficit thinking. Principals and educational leaders can use the following tool to engage faculty in a difficult dialogue designed to expose deficit thinking and move to more positive views of ELLs.

To do this, principals must choose their words carefully. Some principals choose to use collective pronouns such as *we* when they phrase their wording, posing questions such as "What assumptions do we make about parents who do not attend afterschool programs?"

Other principals choose to place the emphasis on the third person, posing questions such as "What assumptions do teachers make about parents who do not attend afterschool programs?"

Sometimes, principals choose to place a modal verb in the sentence, lessening the indictment some teachers might perceive in the sentence: "What assumptions might teachers make about parents who do not attend afterschool programs?"

As the principal, you must gauge your teachers' readiness as you open difficult conversations. In Chapter 3, we discussed ways to address deficit thinking, if it is apparent in faculty comments, through skillful questioning. However, if deficit thinking is embedded and institutionalized, it is sometimes difficult to draw out. This tool is designed to initiate dialogue about potential assumptions that educational leaders and faculty could be making about ELLs, their families, and their communities and help educators talk through the deficit assumptions in an attempt to shift perspectives to an additive view.

As the principal talks through these points with his or her faculty, it is imperative that he or she allow all participants to express themselves. The principal must gauge the climate of the school and weigh the benefits of full-group disclosure and participation with the safety of personal reflection or small groups. In groups in

> **CONSIDER THIS**
>
> *You might be wondering whether it is a good idea to bring up negative liabilities. Yes. If you do not openly address and then explicitly deconstruct negative perceptions of ELLs, the perceptions—often based on stereotypes or assumptions—can persist. In an early professional development session we conducted, we interviewed an ELL who immigrated to the United States as a middle school student, enrolled in pre-advanced placement classes, graduated from high school, was admitted to college, and was experiencing great success. After the session—which we thought was a great success—some teachers commented to me, "Well, he is an exception," or "That is just a fluke." The pervasive impressions of failure for students with identities similar to this student's—ELL, Latino, immigrant, and so forth—overrode the new identity of high expectations and success in spite of proof of possibility.*

which we have assisted dialogues, we have found that the principals who have the greatest success are those who know their faculty and are able to gauge their reactions, vary formats, and provide consistency of themes in ongoing dialogues throughout the year in the varying formats (one-on-one meetings, team meetings, small groups, faculty meetings, personal reflections, whole-group dialogues, think-pair-share, etc.).

TOOL 3.1 ENGAGING IN DIFFICULT DIALOGUES EXAMPLE

Question and Method of Delivery	Examples of Dialogue
What liabilities might teachers perceive English language learners (ELLs) to have? [All teachers wrote these liabilities on sticky notes individually. Next, the principal instructed the teachers to work in groups of four to compare their sticky notes and group them. Teachers grouped identical or similar liabilities together, categorizing or renaming similar liabilities. The principal had not yet decided if she would open the small group discussion to the whole group, but as she monitored the small groups, she noticed the groups generally came up with the same or similar liabilities. She decided it would be powerful to emphasize this and did draw this forward into the whole group for discussion.] If the faculty had perceived diverse liabilities that were based on similar assumptions—but that the faculty perceived as different liabilities—the principal did not want to generate new perceived liabilities and draw these forward as an unintended consequence of the activity. The activity did not take this direction, however, so she did draw it forward to a whole-group activity.	**Examples of individual responses included:** failing Texas Assessment of Academic Skills (accountability test), unmotivated, absent a lot, move too much, don't speak English, parents don't speak English, parents work long hours, sometimes they are in gangs, poverty, they drop out, just don't care about school, engage in risky behavior. **Categories included:** • high poverty rate, • high mobility rate, • high dropout rate, • high failure rate, • high retention rate, • low passing rate on high-stakes tests, • low attendance, • low parental involvement, and • low extracurricular involvement.

Question and Method of Delivery	Examples of Dialogue
What assumptions might these teachers make about ELLs with these perceived liabilities? [For this activity, the principal chose to work from the categories that the whole group had discussed. Each small group worked on each category, discussing assumptions made about ELLs. The principal also chose to keep in third person, giving faculty members the ability to discuss the issues without making it so personal that there was the temptation to be defensive. Her goal was to move forward and move beyond. Knowing her faculty, and the leadership style she had in place, she believed this was best. We have talked with other principals who have used a more direct approach with great success. A third-person approach also works well if your campus is experiencing a demographic shift and your ELL population is beginning to grow.] The principal sat in on one round of discussion for each category. She gave each group a varying amount of time to discuss each category. The times varied because she noted that some of the teachers began repeating assumptions as they moved to the latter categories. After each table discussed each category, the principal debriefed the small-group discussions in a whole-group discussion.	**During the discussion about assumptions teachers made about ELLs with the perceived liability of "high poverty rate," teachers in a small group made these comments:** • Well, we assume parents work long hours or odd hours because ELLs often represent demographics of poverty, but I find that it really just depends on the student. Some of my students have moms who stay home. Some of them, their parents arrange their work hours so that there is a parent at home all the time. Some of them are from single-parent homes, and sometimes they have to take care of their younger siblings, but not all of them. I just get frustrated, as a teacher, because we make assumptions that just because a student might come from poverty that all family values go out the window. That just isn't true. • Sometimes we think that students or parents are caught up in their lives—like helping their families, paying bills, working, or whatever. They are too busy making ends meet to care about education. But that might not be the case. We assume that for them, but we never talk to them—I mean really find out. I don't mean talk to them in a pointed or judgmental way. I mean we don't build a real relationship with them or even talk to them until there is a problem.

(Continued)

TOOL 3.1 ENGAGING IN DIFFICULT DIALOGUES EXAMPLE (Continued)

Question and Method of Delivery	Examples of Dialogue
CONSIDER THIS *During the discussions, the principal asked the question, "What assumptions do teachers make," but many teachers answered with "We assume. . . . " Why is this approach effective? What are potential pitfalls? How can you prepare to avoid them?* In the column to the right, we summarize one small group discussion regarding "high poverty rate" and note bullet points of the whole-group discussion. As teachers talked, the principal was planning her next move. She wanted to use the teachers' comments to shift the focus to the positive and to the planning phase. This first phase was critical. It provided the principal valuable insight into the teachers' beliefs, and it gave the teachers a forum to voice and talk through their beliefs. Also, as they voiced their beliefs and concerns, they became tangible. Until they became tangible, the principal would not be able to move the culture to a culture of high expectations or to a culture of high achievement because the faculty would not explicitly address the deficit assumptions.	**In the debrief, teachers talked through their conclusions:** • We tend to make up reasons for parents or students doing or not doing something based on our experiences, without ever really finding out the real reasons. The parents don't come, so we quit expecting the parents to come, and we don't find out why. We just kind of shrug our shoulders and think, "Oh well. The other parents come, so something must be wrong with these other parents, right?" • We also tend to be a little afraid. And that is based on an assumption of fear—we are afraid that this population is going to cause us to miss certain accountability goals—dropout rates, retention rates, testing rates, language acquisition rates, and so forth. This is a new challenge, and we assume that if they would just work a little harder, they would get it—whatever that goal is we are trying to reach. We have made it into a bottom line. What is important to us is meeting that bottom line—whatever the accountability line is. We assume that is important to our students . . . and honestly, it probably isn't the one and only reason they are in school. We never asked what is important to them. What do they want? College? We never even talk about it. Honors classes? Forget it, let's pass this test or this class and breathe a sigh of relief!

120

Question and Method of Delivery	Examples of Dialogue
	• We make the assumption that failure is the expectation and mediocrity is the best achievement they are capable of. When they reach what we consider the minimum expectation for other students, we celebrate.
CONSIDER THIS *What makes an assumption, an assumption is that we never think about—or interrogate—it. This is what makes it seem logical or just the way it is and is what can make changing school cultures difficult. Principals can't build new, positive school cultures without deconstructing or reconstructing toxic ones. Which do you anticipate will be the hardest assumptions to bring to the surface?*	
We shared that we make assumptions because we don't have the necessary perspectives. How can we change or broaden our perspectives? [Because the principal wanted teachers to start to think outside the box, she decided to engage teachers in think-pair-share. She altered the traditional strategy a bit, combining it with another partnering strategy. She gave both partners thirty seconds to brainstorm and make notes. Then, in pairs, partner A talked for sixty seconds while partner B listened. Partner A	**The ideas from the whole-group discussion included:** • Hold parent meetings at times that are convenient to ELL parents, and in the parents' native languages, to discuss issues. Personally invite the parents—by either a phone call (from a translator) or a home visit (accompanied by a translator)—to enlist initial parental buy-in. While teachers were not yet sure what would motivate or encourage parents to come, programs in which their children were involved were other possibilities. They were brainstorming ideas and were willing to try several if some didn't work.

(Continued)

TOOL 3.1 ENGAGING IN DIFFICULT DIALOGUES EXAMPLE (Continued)

Question and Method of Delivery	Examples of Dialogue
shared the ideas he or she brainstormed. If he or she ran out of ideas, he or she could continue to brainstorm and jot down the new ideas. After sixty seconds, partner B shared his or her ideas. If he or she ran out of ideas, he or she could elaborate ideas either partner shared. At the end of these sixty seconds, partners A and B had two minutes to engage in dialogue to elaborate, strengthen, combine, or modify their ideas. After two minutes, the teachers talked in small groups to bring together their ideas, and then the principal brought it to whole-group discussion.]	• At the meetings—which they thought they wanted to call something else, perhaps "forums"—they would get parent input on issues. They would also be able to explain goals and objectives related to parental involvement. • The faculty showed great interest in talking with the students, parents, and community about goals for their youth.
What opportunities might we have missed?	**Excerpt of notes from tablets:**
[At this point, the principal wanted to keep the momentum of the dialogue. She also felt that the faculty would benefit from the energy of whole-group participation. She decided to open this to the whole group and enlisted two scribes. This was a common practice at faculty meetings. Two scribes (different every time) would record the faculty's thoughts as they brainstormed possible missed opportunities. The faculty was in the habit of bringing their easels and large tablet paper to faculty meetings. There were about ten at the front of the room in which they were meeting. At the end of the initial discussion, they had filled all ten tablets with their raw thoughts. The scribes returned to their seats, and the principal then guided the faculty in a discussion to consolidate, group, debrief, and discuss the thoughts on the tablets. As they did, the principal	[Teachers noted that they would be able to better answer this question once they took a more responsive approach to students, but many teachers who were responsive to students and parents shared, and those who planned to become more responsive were still able to build on what they knew about their students.]

Question and Method of Delivery	Examples of Dialogue
made conclusive notes on the white board at the front of the room. These notes were the general statements of missed opportunities. As the principal was writing, she was phrasing the notes knowing she would use them to guide the next question.]	
CONSIDER THIS *As the faculty continued to talk, the principal noticed she and the teachers were speaking in generalities. For the time being, she felt this was appropriate because the goal of the exercise was to move the teachers beyond negative perceptions of students and move to a focus on students' assets. However, she became worried that a focus on generalities could open the door for teachers to begin (or continue) to stereotype students. How can the principal encourage her faculty to begin (or continue) to see each ELL as an individual and encourage teachers to know students individually?*	**CONSIDER THIS** *Once the teachers began talking, the principal noticed that many of their comments, such as ELLs are "hard workers" or ELLs' families have a "strong sense of home," stood in direct contrast to some of the earlier, more negative comments. Why is this? What happened? Did the students change? How did the principal ethically facilitate the dialogue to move the faculty to a more positive perspective? How can school leaders craft positive, engaging, two-way dialogues that achieve this goal?*

(Continued)

TOOL 3.1 ENGAGING IN DIFFICULT DIALOGUES EXAMPLE (Continued)

Question and Method of Delivery	Examples of Dialogue
	Strong sense of community and "home"; profound faith in the "American dream" and opportunity—especially with newcomer students; strong community networks are in place—businesses, churches; once you win their trust, they are very loyal; hard workers; they deeply care about getting ahead; their families put a lot of hope in their students—their family's legacy in their children's hands; they are almost like a blank slate—not that they don't come here with their own culture and language and hopes, but they are so open to learning, and I find it very inspiring; they are emergent bilingual and sometimes trilingual or multilingual students; many of them immigrated here (either recently or a generation or two ago) for social mobility, and they want to achieve that—education can give them that—that is an opportunity we have to offer; they want to learn English, and they are so motivated to learn English—I don't think we missed that opportunity completely, but I think we aren't there yet.
	Conclusive notes:
	• Our ELL students have strong community and home networks.
	• Our ELL students have intense motivation for upward social/economic movement.
	• For ELL students, education and English acquisition are a means for social/economic movement and increased opportunity.
	• Our students are emergent bi-, tri-, and multilingual students.

Question and Method of Delivery	Examples of Dialogue
How can we support our students' assets? [The principal gave each small group two to three minutes to digest these four conclusive statements and discuss how they can support these assets. The principal wanted to emphasize to the faculty how these four attributes were particular to the ELL population. The faculty has seen the ELL population as at risk since the population entered the school, and a paradigm shift was needed. This phase of the discussion was critical, and the principal knew this phase would be ongoing. After two to three minutes, the principal posed the question to the whole group and again used the same format as she used for the previous question, keeping the four conclusive notes on the white board.]	**Reach out to their networks instead of expecting them to come to ours. Then we can get information out about school events.** One teacher said, "Then, we can build a bridge between the community and the academic networks. We expect them to build an entirely new network with us, but we never took the time to go to them. They are already doing double the work at school—learning English and academic content—yet here we are expecting them to do double the work outside of school, too?" **Offer information about postsecondary opportunities—either college or career opportunities.** One teacher said, "Right now, it is all about what is on the immediate horizon—testing and the current grade. We aren't making a map to the future. If students and their families are looking for social and economic mobility, then it makes sense that all this business about passing isn't beneficial when it isn't fit into the larger picture. We have to put it into the larger picture and help make a plan for their goals and look beyond short-term goals." **Encourage first language use and offer information about current needs of bilingual workers with their first language in the current job market.**

TOOL 3.2 ENGAGING IN DIFFICULT DIALOGUES TEMPLATE

Question and Method	Discussion
1. What liabilities might teachers perceive ELLs to have?	
2. What assumptions might these teachers make about ELLs with these perceived liabilities?	
3. How can we change our perspectives?	
4. What opportunities might we have missed?	
5. How can we support our students' assets?	

TOOL 3.3 LANGUAGE PROFICIENCY LEVELS QUICK REFERENCE GUIDE

Preproduction		Early Production	
Characteristics	Student Needs	Characteristics	Student Needs
• Silent period • Beginning to understand English when they hear it but not yet ready to use it verbally • 0–6 months • Up to 500 words in receptive vocabulary • May repeat key words or phrases but not verbally producing language	• Extensive graphic support • Highly contextualized, concrete learning opportunities • Safe, friendly, supportive environment • Opportunities for heavily scaffolded participation in class activities—at their readiness levels • Targeted first-language support for content-related objectives • Formative assessments modified to offer students either/or choices with graphic supports so students can show comprehension of content	• Beginning to come out of their perceived shells • Not only understanding English (reading and listening) but producing English (writing and speaking) • Minimal comprehension • Up to 1,000 words in receptive and productive vocabulary • Beginning to speak and write in short, one- to two-word phrases, often in response to direct questions	• Continued support as described for students in preproduction stage • Prepared sentence stems, enabling students to accurately show their content knowledge while also building academic language • Participation in choral reading of content-related texts • Very structured opportunities for language production within content • Extensive use of graphic organizers • Access to modified supplementary texts

(Continued)

127

TOOL 3.3 LANGUAGE PROFICIENCY LEVELS QUICK REFERENCE GUIDE (Continued)

Speech Emergence		Intermediate Fluency	
Characteristics	Student Needs	Characteristics	Student Needs
• About 3,000 words in receptive and productive vocabulary • Beginning to initiate speech and produce questions • Comprehension begins to increase exponentially • Beginning to write brief stories and paragraphs	• Continued support as described above with decreasing scaffolds • Continued graphic and video support for comprehension and assessment • Participate in paired or small-group reading • Opportunities to journal in English (provide extensive, less-structured production activities)	• About 6,000 words in receptive and productive vocabulary • Beginning to produce more complex sentence structures • Initiating questions • Better able to transfer metacognitive skills to comprehend content because they are no longer in survival mode • Still often cognitively processing in native language	• Language production still contains many errors—continued encouragement to produce language, very targeted corrections so students continue to produce language • Increased emphasis on higher-order thinking skills • Increased emphasis on developing metacognitive comprehension strategies • Continued scaffolds to support comprehension and assessment • Additional processing time for comprehension and assessment

Advanced fluency	
Characteristics	**Student Needs**
• Near-native ability in English • Still developing academic language proficiency • Can take as long as 5–7 years or more to fully develop advanced academic fluency	• Students may have been exited from limited English proficiency services—continued support in developing academic language proficiency • Continued graphic support, engagement, and semantic mapping to continue language development

TOOL 3.4 QUICK REFERENCE GUIDE MODIFICATIONS FOR ENGLISH LANGUAGE LEARNERS (ELLS)

Accommodation/Modification X = appropriate scaffold x = appropriate as a transitional scaffold	Preproduction	Early Production	Intermediate Fluency	Advanced Fluency
Give tests orally	X	X	x	x
Strategically use native-language support	X	X	X	x
Use bilingual dictionary	X	X	X	x
Preteach academic vocabulary	X	X	X	X
Reduce assignments in English	X	X	x	
Give instructions orally and in writing	X	X	X	X
Provide summaries of texts in English for preview and review	X	X	X	x
Provide native-language summaries for preview and review	X	X	x	
Allow extra time to complete assignments in English	X	X	X	x
Assess comprehension via demonstration through visuals, drawings	X	X		
Assess comprehension through alternative means (retellings, orally)		X	x	
Provide concrete, real-world examples of academic material	X	X	X	x
Use linguistically accommodated texts	X	X	x	
Use linguistically accommodated assessments	X	X	x	

Accommodation/Modification

X = appropriate scaffold x = appropriate as a transitional scaffold	Preproduction	Early Production	Intermediate Fluency	Advanced Fluency
Use graphic organizers	X	X	X	X
Use anecdotal records as a form of assessment	X	X	X	x
Keep portfolio of work as a form of assessment	X	X	X	X
Provide sentence stems for ELLs' written responses	X	X		
Provide sentence stems for ELLs' oral responses		X	x	
Think-pair-share during instruction	x	X	X	X
Utilize small-group, interactive learning	X	X	X	X
Incorporate visuals into content lessons	X	X	X	X
Allow sufficient wait time for oral responses	X	X	X	X
Provide hands-on materials and manipulatives	X	X	X	X
Provide frequent opportunities for student-to-student interaction	X	X	X	X
Provide frequent opportunities for student-to-teacher interaction	X	X	X	X
Provide frequent opportunities for student written reflection	X	X	X	X
Allow graphic either/or options for students to choose as an alternative to oral assessment	X			

CHAPTER 4 TOOLS

Tool 4.1 Assessing Faculty Content Knowledge

Tool 4.1 guides the first steps in assessing the faculty's professional development needs. It is important to first assess faculty needs and then prioritize these needs to develop a comprehensive plan of action. This assessment, combined with walk-throughs, provides powerful insight into faculty professional development needs.

Tool 4.2 Working Together to Plan and Implement Language Objectives

In support teams, the English as a second language teacher or another faculty leader can help provide assistance in developing language objectives to augment content objectives. In addition, the support teams can work together to share strategies, discuss how to implement strategies, and evaluate strategy implementation. Teacher leaders of support teams can use Tool 4.2 to guide the process of implementation.

Tool 4.3 Peer Coaching Observation and Reflection Guide

Teachers use Tool 4.3, Peer Coaching Observation and Reflection Guide, to take notes while observing a lesson. The guide provides a nonevaluative way for teachers to make notes about the strategy a teacher tries.

Tool 4.4 Walk-Through Guide for Principals

The Walk-Through Guide is meant not as an evaluative tool but as an observational tool to guide the need for individual-faculty and whole-faculty professional development. As a walk-through tool, it can be used in parts. The principal may not observe all tools on the guide depending on when the walk-through takes place. The guide would be used in a similar fashion as the coaching and reflection guide—as a guide for individual teacher development of knowledge and skills related to best practices for teaching ELLs.

TOOL 4.1 ASSESSING FACULTY CONTENT KNOWLEDGE

General Subject	Faculty Knowledge of Specific Topics	√	Faculty Understanding of Implications for Practice	√
Basic Linguistic Knowledge	• phonemes, morphemes, syntax • semantics, pragmatics		• how to capitalize on positive transfer from first language to second language • how to teach appropriate social language use within content	
Language Acquisition Process	• social language development as compared to academic language development • Krashen and Terrell's (1983) theory of second-language acquisition • common difficulties in second language acquisition negative transfer		• how to provide opportunities for oral language within the content • how to build on student's prior knowledge of content and first language to continue to build and develop content and second language • how to recognize natural errors as students acquire second language • how to promote second-language use in a positive, welcoming manner • how to use cognates to access prior knowledge	
Foundational Instruction and Assessment Strategies for English Language Learners (ELLs)	• integrating literacy and language objectives into content areas • use of immediate/formative assessments for ELLs • using manipulatives in content areas • developing oral language through content • providing comprehensible input • making text accessible to ELLs		• how to differentiate language objectives and content objectives • how to align appropriate assessment and evaluation with content objectives • how to avoid grading students down for language errors if not explicitly taught language objectives • how to appropriately respond to language errors, building language proficiency without hindering student language use	
Basic Literacy Skills Information	• the five literacy skills • using literacy skills effectively in all content areas		• how to incorporate multiple literacy experiences in one instructional or assessment activity	

TOOL 4.2 WORKING TOGETHER TO PLAN AND IMPLEMENT LANGUAGE OBJECTIVES

Steps	Purpose	
Assess	Discuss areas of instructional concern or English language learner instructional needs.	
Set Goals	Identify specific student needs and determine the required skill or strategy. Identify specific strategies or practices from professional development for teachers to implement for improvement.	
Prepare	Collaboratively plan for the instructional activities and strategies. Create a model lesson plan together. Identify specific language objectives needed to augment the content objectives.	
Implement	Teach the lesson. If possible, have the support team observe the lesson. At minimum, the English as a second language teacher or teacher leaders should observe the lesson.	
Reflect	After teaching the lesson, the support team reflects on these questions: • What went well? + • What can we do differently next time? Δ • What was the effect on student learning and engagement?	

TOOL 4.3 PEER COACHING OBSERVATION AND REFLECTION GUIDE—FOR PEER COACHES

Planning and Standards

What content objective does the instruction address?

+   ◁

What language objectives are integrated into the content?

+   ◁

How do the content and language objective complement each other?

+   ◁

Lesson Implementation

Strategy tried:

+   ◁

Strategy tried:

+   ◁

Student Engagement and Learning—How were English language learners given access to

- multiple literacy experiences (reading, writing, listening, speaking)?

+   ◁

- high expectations and rigor?

+   ◁

- active engagement in learning?

+   ◁

- ongoing assessment of their content and language learning?

+   ◁

TOOL 4.4 WALK-THROUGH GUIDE FOR PRINCIPALS

Teacher: _____ Date: _____ Subject: _____ Grade: _____

	+	△
Standards		
Content objective clear and aligned with state standards		
Language objective clear and aligned with state's English language proficiency standards		
Accessing Prior Knowledge	+	△
Access or build prior knowledge		
Vocabulary	+	△
Explicitly teach vocabulary		
Explicitly teach language features (cognates, idioms, etc.)		
Engagement	+	△
All students actively engaged		
Students provided multiple literacy experiences • Speaking • Listening • Reading • Writing		
Content	+	△
Scaffolds in place to achieve high expectations		
Rigor in place for content		
Assessment	+	△
Ongoing, formative assessment of content		
Ongoing, formative assessment of language		
Assessment appropriate for language proficiency level		

References

Achieve. (2009). *Closing the expectations gap.* Washington, DC: Author.

Adelman, C. (1999). *Answers in the tool box: Academic intensity, attendance patterns, and bachelor's degree attainment.* Retrieved September 21, 2001, from http://www.ed.gov/pubs/Toolbox/Title.html

Arbuckle, M. (1997). Leadership for professional development: Essential arenas of work and learning. In S. D. Caldwell (Ed.), *Professional development in learning centered schools* (pp. 168–184). Oxford, OH: National Staff Development Council.

Batalova, J., Fix, M., & Murray, J. (2007). *Measures of change: The demography and literacy of adolescent English learners.* Washington, DC: Migration Policy Institute.

Bauch, P. (2001). School-community partnership in rural schools: Leadership, renewal, and a sense of place. *Peabody Journal of Education, 76*(2), 204–222.

Bellamy, G. T., Fulmer, C. L., Murphy, M. J., & Muth, R. (2007). *Principal accomplishments: How school leaders succeed.* New York: Teachers College Press.

Bellamy, P. C. (Ed.). (2005). *Seeing with new eyes.* Portland, OR: Northwest Regional Educational Laboratory.

Bennis, W. (1989). *On becoming a leader.* New York: Basic Books.

Berra, Y., & Kaplan, D. (2001). *When you come to a fork in the road, take it.* New York: Hyperion.

Bloom, B. S., Englehart, M. D., Furst, E. J., Hill, W. H., & Krathwohl, D. R. (1956). *Taxonomy of educational objectives: The classification of educational goals. Handbook I: Cognitive domain.* New York: David McKay.

Buehl, D. (2001). *Classroom strategies for interactive learning.* Newark, DE: International Reading Association.

Calderón, M. (2007). *Teaching reading to English language learners: A framework for improving achievement in content areas.* Thousand Oaks: CA: Corwin.

Chenoweth, K. (2009). *How it's being done: Urgent lessons from unexpected schools.* Cambridge, MA: Harvard Education Press.

Chubb, J., & Loveless, T. (2002). Bridging the achievement gap. In J. Chubb & T. Loveless (Eds.), *Bridging the achievement gap* (pp. 1–11). Washington, DC: Brookings Institution.

College Board. (2006). *Advanced placement report to the nation: 2006.* Retrieved January 20, 2011, from http://www.collegeboard.com/prod_downloads/about/news_info/ap/2006/2006_ap-report-nation.pdf

Collins, J. (2001). *Good to great: Why some companies make the leap . . . and others don't.* New York: HarperCollins.

Conley, D. T. (2007). *Redefining college readiness.* Eugene, OR: Educational Policy Improvement Center.

Conyers, J., & Ewy, R. (2004). *Charting your course: Lessons learned during the journey toward performance excellence.* Milwaukee, WI: ASQ Quality Press.

Council for Corporate and School Partnerships. (2002). *Guiding principles for school-business partnerships.* Washington, DC: Author.

Cuban, L., Lichtenstein, G., Evenchik, A., Tombari, M., & Pozzoboni, K. (2010). *Against the odds: Insights from one district's small school reform.* Cambridge, MA: Harvard Education Press.

Cubitt, S., Irvine, R., & Dow, A. (1999). *Top tools for social science teachers.* Auckland, New Zealand: Addison Wesley Longman.

Dantley, M. E. (2005). Moral leadership: Shifting the management paradigm. In F. W. English (Ed.), *The Sage handbook of educational leadership: Advances in theory, research, and practice* (pp. 34–46). Thousand Oaks, CA: Sage.

Darling-Hammond, L., La Pointe, M., Meyerson, D., & Orr, M. T. (2007). *Preparing school leaders for a changing world: Lessons from exemplary leadership development programs. School Leadership Study: Executive Summary.* Palo Alto, CA: Stanford University.

Deal, T. E., & Peterson, K. D. (2009). *Shaping school culture* (2nd ed.). San Francisco: Jossey-Bass.

de Jong, E. J., & Harper, C. A. (2008). ESL is good teaching "plus": Preparing standard curriculum teachers for all learners. In M. E. Brisk (Ed.), *Language, culture, and community in teacher education* (pp. 127–148). Mahwah, NJ: Lawrence Erlbaum.

Donaldson, G. A., Jr. (2006). *Cultivating leadership in schools: Connecting people, purpose, and practice* (2nd ed.). New York: Teachers College Press.

Donaldson, G. A., Jr. (2008). *How leaders learn: Cultivating capacities for school improvement.* New York: Teachers College Press.

Duffy, F. M. (2004). *Moving upward together: Creating strategic alignment to sustain systemic school improvement.* Lanham, MD: Scarecrow Press.

Earley, P., & Bubb, S. (2004). *Leading and managing continuing professional development.* Thousand Oaks, CA: Sage.

Echevarria, J., & Graves, A. (2007). *Sheltered content instruction: Teaching English language learners with diverse abilities.* Boston: Pearson.

Edelman, M. W. (1992). *The measure of our success.* New York: HarperCollins.

Editorial Projects in Education Research Center. (2009). *Perspectives on a population: English-language learners in American schools.* Bethesda, MD: Author.

Editorial Projects in Education Research Center. (2010). *Diplomas count.* Bethesda, MD: Author.

Elmore, R. F. (2000). *Building a new structure for school leadership.* Washington, DC: Albert Shanker Institute.

Elmore, R. F. (2005). *School reform from the inside out: Policy, practice, and performance.* Cambridge, MA: Harvard Educational Review.

Epstein, J. L., Sanders, M. G., Sheldon, S. B., Simon, B. S., Clark Salinas, K., Rodriguez Jansorn, N., et al. (2002). *School, family, and community partnerships: Your handbook for action* (2nd ed.). Thousand Oaks, CA: Corwin.

Fairbairn, S., & Jones-Vo, S. (2010). *Differentiating instruction and assessment for English language learners: A guide for K–12 teachers.* Philadelphia: Caslon.

Flanary, R. (2007, August). *Conversation.* Shared at the National Council of Professors of Educational Administration board meeting, Chicago.

Freeman, D., & Freeman, Y. (2007). *English language learners: The essential guide.* New York: Scholastic.

Fullan, M. (1993). *Challenge forces: Probing the depths of educational reform.* Briton, PA: Falmer.

Fullan, M. (2001). *Leading in a culture of change.* San Francisco: Jossey-Bass.

Fullan, M. (2005). *Leadership and sustainability: System thinkers in action.* Thousand Oaks, CA: Corwin.

Fullan, M. (2007). *The new meaning of educational change.* New York: Teachers College Press.

Fullan, M. (2009). *The challenge of change: Start school improvement now!* (2nd ed.). Thousand Oaks, CA: Corwin.

Fullan, M., Hill, P., & Crevola, C. (2006). *Breakthrough.* Thousand Oaks, CA: Corwin.

Gandara, P. (2008). Immigrants and English learners: Can multiple pathways smooth their paths? In J. Oakes & M. Saunders (Eds.), *Beyond tracking: Multiple pathways to college, career, and civic participation* (pp. 71–86). Cambridge, MA: Harvard Education Press.

Gandara, P., & Contreras, F. (2009). *The Latino education crisis: The consequences of failed social practices.* Cambridge, MA: Harvard University Press.

Gladieux, L. E., & Swail, W. S. (1998). Financial aid is not enough: Improving the odds of college success. *College Board Review, 185,* 1–11.

Glathorn, A. A., & Fox, L. E. (1996). *Quality teaching through professional development.* Thousand Oaks, CA: Corwin.

Hall, G. E., & Hord, S. M. (2001). *Implementing change: Patterns, principles, and potholes.* Needham, MA: Allyn & Bacon.

Hamayan, E., & Freeman, R. (2006). *English language learners at school: A guide for administrators.* Philadelphia: Caslon.

Henderson, A., & Mapp, K. (2002). *A new wave of evidence: The impact of school, family, and community connections on student achievement.* Austin, TX: Southwest Educational Development Laboratory.

Herman, J. L., Aschbacher, P. R., & Winters, L. (1992). *A practical guide to alternative assessment.* Alexandria, VA: Association for Supervision and Curriculum Development.

Horowitz, A. R., Uro, G., Price-Baugh, R., Simon, C., Uzzell, R., Lewis, S., et al. (2009). *Succeeding with English language learners: Lessons learned from the Great City schools.* Washington, DC: Council of the Great City Schools.

Kagan, S. (1992). *Cooperative learning.* San Juan Capistrano, CA: Resources for Teachers.

Kagan, S., & Kagan, M. (1998). *Multiple intelligences: The complete MI book.* San Clemente, CA: Kagan.

Kandel-Cisco, B., & Padron, Y. (2008). Using a resiliency perspective to inform bilingual teachers' classroom inquiry. In M. Cowart (Ed.), *Current issues and best practice in bilingual and ESL education* (pp. 237–261). Denton: Texas Woman's University: Federation of North Texas Universities.

Kinnucan-Welsch, K., & Jenlink, P. (2005). Conversation and the development of learning communities. In B. H. Banathy & P. M. Jenlink (Eds.), *Dialogue as a means of collective communication* (pp. 393–426). New York: Kluwer Academic/Plenum.

Kozol, J. (2001, February). *Keynote address.* Presented at the National Conference of Education, American Association of School Administrators, Orlando, FL.

Krashen, S. D. (1982). *Principles and practice in second language acquisition.* Oxford, UK: Pergamon.

Krashen, S. D., & Terrell, T. D. (1983). *The natural approach: Language acquisition in the classroom.* Hayward, CA: Alemany Press.

Lambert, L., Walker, D., Zimmerman, D. P., Cooper, J. E., Lambert, M. D., Gardner, M. E., et al. (1995). *The constructivist leader.* New York: Teachers College Press.

La Plant, J. (1997). The principal's role and staff development. In S. D. Caldwell (Ed.), *Professional development in learning centered schools* (pp. 50–63). Oxford, OH: National Staff Development Council.

Leithwood, K., Seashore Louis, K., Anderson, S., & Wahlstrom, D. (2004). *How leadership influences student learning.* New York: Center for Applied Research and Education Improvement, University of Minnesota, Ontario Institute for Studies in Education at the University of Ontario, and the Wallace Foundation.

Leithwood, K. A., & Riehl, C. (2005). What do we already know about educational leadership? In W. A. Firestone & C. Riehl (Eds.), *A new agenda for research in educational leadership* (pp. 12–27). New York: Teachers College Press.

Lindsey, D., Martinez, R., & Lindsey, R. (2007). *Culturally proficient coaching: Supporting educators to create equitable schools.* Thousand Oaks, CA: Corwin.

Lucido, F., & McEachern, W. (2000). The influence of bilingualism on reading scores. *Reading Improvement, 37*(2), 87–91.

Matthews, L. J., & Crow, G. M. (2003). *Being and becoming a principal: Role conceptions for contemporary principals and assistant principals.* Boston: Pearson Education.

McDonough, P. (2008, May). *Session presentation.* Presented at the Texas State Gear-Up Conference, McAllen, TX.

Melendez, T. (2010a, February). *Keynote address.* Presented at the National Association for Bilingual Education. Retrieved September 7, 2010, from www2.ed.gov/news/speeches/2010/02/02032010.html

Melendez, T. (2010b, March). *Keynote address.* Presented at the College Board Prepárate Conference, San Diego, CA.

Menken, K., & Antunez, B. (2001). *An overview of the preparation and certification of teachers working with limited English proficient students.* Washington, DC: National Clearinghouse of Bilingual Education. Retrieved June 28, 2009, from http://www.ericsp.org/pages/digests/ncbe.pdf

Monroe, L. (2000, October). *Keynote address.* Presented at the Center for Professional Development and Technology fall conference, Stephen F. Austin State University, Nacogdoches, TX.

Murphy, J. (2005). *Connecting teacher leadership and school improvement.* Thousand Oaks, CA: Corwin.

National Association of Partners in Education. (2001). *Creating, managing and sustaining school-community-business partnerships: A collaborative, consensus-building approach.* Alexandria, VA: Author.

National Clearinghouse for English Language Acquisition. (2008). *Education English language learners: Building teacher capacity* (Vol. 3). Retrieved March 3, 2009, from http://www.ncela.gwu.edu/files/uploads/3/EducatingELLsBuildingTeacherCapacityVol3.pdf

National Clearinghouse for English Language Acquisition. (2010). *Language minorities, languages, English (second language), limited English speaking, population,*

Spanish speaking. Retrieved March 3, 2009, from http://www.ncela.gwu.edu/faqs/

National Commission on the High School Senior Year. (2001, October). *Raising our sights: No high school senior left behind.* Princeton, NJ: Woodrow Wilson National Fellowship Foundation.

National Staff Development Council. (2004). *Standards for staff development* (Rev. ed.). Oxford, OH: Author.

Negroni, P. (2002). A network of relationships. *Phi Delta Kappan, 84*(4), 284–285.

Nieto, S. (1999). *The light in their eyes.* New York: Teachers College Press.

No Child Left Behind Act of 2001. Pub. L. No. 107-110. Title III: Language instruction for limited English proficient and immigrant students.

Noddings, N. (1984). *Caring: A feminine approach to ethics and moral education.* Berkeley: University of California Press.

Olivos, E. M. (2009). Collaboration with Latino families: A critical perspective. *Intervention in School and Clinic, 45*(2), 109–115.

Osterman, K. F., & Kottkamp, R. B. (2004). *Reflective practice for educators: Professional development to student learning.* Thousand Oaks, CA: Corwin.

Pellicer, L. O. (1999). *Caring enough to lead: How reflective practice leads to moral leadership.* Thousand Oaks, CA: Corwin.

Pena, D. C. (2000). Parent involvement: Influencing factors and limitations. *Journal of Educational Research, 94*(1), 42–54.

Randall, D. (1969). "The ballad of Birmingham." Retrieved May 17, 2010, from http://webinstituteforteachers.org/~vfjohnson/ballbham.html

Reyes, P., Scribner, J. D., & Paredes Scribner, A. (1999). *Lessons from high-performing Hispanic schools.* New York: Teachers College Press.

Reyes, P., & Wagstaff, L. (2005). How does leadership promote successful teaching and learning for diverse students? In W. Firestone & C. Riehl (Eds.), *A new agenda for research in educational leadership* (pp. 101–118). New York: Teachers College Press.

Reynolds, A. (1991). *Bilingualism, multiculturalism, and second language learning.* Hillsdale, NJ: Lawrence Erlbaum.

Robles-Goodwin, P. J. (2006). Understanding English language learners: Challenges and promises. In P. Dam & M. T. Cowart (Eds.), *Cultural and linguistic issues for English language learners* (pp. 56–82). San Marcos, TX: Canh Nam.

Scheurich, J. J., & Skrla, L. (2003). *Leadership for equity and excellence: Creating high-achievement classrooms, schools, and districts.* Thousand Oaks, CA: Corwin.

Scheurich, J. J., Skrla, L., & Johnson, J. F. (2000). Think carefully about equity and accountability. *Phi Delta Kappan, 82*(4), 293–299.

Schlechty, P. C. (2001). *Shaking up the school house: How to support and sustain educational innovation.* San Francisco: Jossey-Bass.

Schlechty, P. C. (2008). No community left behind. *Phi Delta Kappan, 89*(8). Retrieved July 1, 2009, from http://www.pdkintl.org/kappan/k_v89/k0804sch.htm

Scribner, J. D., Young, M. D., & Pedroza, A. (1999). Building collaborative relationships with parents. In P. Reyes, J. D. Scribner, & A. Paredes Scribner (Eds.), *Lessons from high performing Hispanic schools: Creating learning communities* (pp. 36–60). Williston, VT: Teachers College Press.

Senge, P. (2006). *The fifth discipline: The art and practice of the learning organization.* New York: Doubleday.

Sergiovanni, T. I. (2007). *Rethinking leadership: A collection of articles* (2nd ed.). Thousand Oaks, CA: Corwin.

Shefelbine, J. R. (2008). An examination of the roles and perspectives of central office supervisors of programs for English language learners. In P. Dam & M. T. Cowart (Eds.), *Current issues and best practice in bilingual and ESL education* (pp. 262–299). Denton: Federation of North Texas Area Universities.

Short, D., & Fitzsimmons, S. (2007). *Double the work: Challenges and solutions to acquiring language and academic literacy for adolescent English language learners— A report to the Carnegie Corporation of New York.* Washington, DC: Alliance for Excellent Education.

Short, P. M., & Greer, J. T. (1997). *Leadership in empowered schools: Themes from innovative efforts.* Upper Saddle River, NJ: Prentice Hall.

Silva, C., Weinburgh, M., Smith, K., Barreto, G., & Gabel, J. (2008). Partnering to develop academic language for English language learners through mathematics and science. *Childhood Education, 85*(2), 107–113.

Slavin, R. E., & Cheung, A. (2005). A synthesis of research on language of reading instruction for English Language Learners. *Review of Educational Research, 75*(2), 247–284.

Sparks, D. (1997). School reform requires a new form of staff development. In S. D. Caldwell (Ed.), *Professional development in learning centered schools* (pp. 2–11). Oxford, OH: National Staff Development Council.

Starratt, R. (2004). *Ethical leadership.* San Francisco: Jossey-Bass.

Suarez-Orozco, C., & Suarez-Orozco, M. M. (2001). *Children of immigration.* Cambridge, MA: Harvard University Press.

Tate, M. L. (2004). *Sit and get won't grow dendrites: Twenty professional learning strategies that engage the adult brain.* Thousand Oaks, CA: Corwin.

Treviño, R. (2000). *Parent involvement and remarkable student achievement: A study of Mexican-origin families of migrant high-achievers.* Doctoral dissertation, University of Texas at Austin.

U.S. Department of Education. (2001). *Paving the way to postsecondary: K–12 intervention programs for underrepresented youth* (NCES Report No. 2001-2005). Washington, DC: National Postsecondary Education Cooperative Access Working Group.

Valencia, R. R. (1997). Conceptualizing the notion of deficit thinking. In R. R. Valencia (Ed.), *The evolution of deficit thinking: Educational thought and practice* (pp. 1–12). New York: Routledge.

Valenzuela, A. (1999). *Subtractive schooling: U.S.-Mexican youth and the politics of caring.* Albany: State University of New York Press.

Vygotsky, L. (1978). Interaction between learning and development. In *Mind in society* (M. Cole, Trans., pp. 79–91). Cambridge, MA: Harvard University Press.

Index

CORWIN
A SAGE Company

The Corwin logo—a raven striding across an open book—represents the union of courage and learning. Corwin is committed to improving education for all learners by publishing books and other professional development resources for those serving the field of PreK–12 education. By providing practical, hands-on materials, Corwin continues to carry out the promise of its motto: **"Helping Educators Do Their Work Better."**

Advancing professional learning for student success

Learning Forward (formerly National Staff Development Council) is an international association of learning educators committed to one purpose in K–12 education: Every educator engages in effective professional learning every day so every student achieves.